MISSILE DEFENCE
ROUND ONE

MISSILE DEFENCE
ROUND ONE

STEVEN STAPLES

JAMES LORIMER & COMPANY LTD., PUBLISHERS
TORONTO

James Lorimer & Company Ltd. acknowledges the support of the Ontario Arts Council. We acknowledge the support of the Government of Canada through the Book Publishing Industry Development Program (BPIDP) for our publishing activities. We acknowledge the support of the Canada Council for the Arts for our publishing program.We acknowledge the support of the Government of Ontario through the Ontario Media Development Corporation's Ontario Book Initiative.

Cover design: Meghan Collins

The Canada Council | Le Conseil des Arts
for the Arts | du Canada

ONTARIO ARTS COUNCIL
CONSEIL DES ARTS DE L'ONTARIO

Library and Archives Canada Cataloguing in Publication
Staples, Steven
    Missile defence: round one / Steven Staples.
Includes index.
ISBN-13: 978-1-55028-929-9
ISBN-10: 1-55028-929-2
        1. Ballistic missile defenses—Canada. 2. Strategic Defense Initiative. 3. Canada—Military relations—United States. 4. United States—Military relations—Canada. 5. Political participation—Canada. I. Title.

UA745.C3S68 2006   358.1'740971   C2006-903632-2

James Lorimer & Company Ltd.,Publishers
317 Adelaide Street West, Suite 1002
Toronto, Ontario, M5V 1P9
www.lorimer.ca

Printed and bound in Canada.

Photo credits: t=top, b=bottom
Charlottetown Guardian: 135t; Jane Chytilova: 133b; CP/Tom Hansen: 133t; Shelagh Corbett/Pilot Design Studio: 132; Ottawa Citizen: 131t; Steven Staples: 131b, 134, 135b; Amy Thompson: 136b

CONTENTS

For Caroline

ACKNOWLEDGEMENTS

I would like to thank all of those who provided so much valuable support and advice for this book and the campaign that it is about: Janet Shorten, Sara Kemp, Tony Clarke, Debbie Grisdale, Mel Hurtig, Peggy Mason, Peter Coombes, Jillian Skeet, Anil Naidoo, Mel Watkins, Bruce Campbell, Maude Barlow, Douglas Roche, Ernie Regehr, Murray Dobbin, Michael Byers, Sarah Estabrooks, Alexa McDonough, Anthony Salloum, Mike Wallace, Kathleen Ruff, Tamara Lorincz (my co-recipient of the 2005 international Peace in Space Award), Loc Dao, Lara Kroeker, Steven Shrybman, Matthew Good, Alice Slater, Franz Hartmann, Jennifer Simons, Cynda Collins-Arsenault, Paul Carroll, my publisher James Lorimer and his talented staff, and the many thousands of Canadians who signed letters, made phone calls, sent donations, gave presentations, held placards, organized meetings, and participated in the campaign in so many ways.

A special thanks to my wife Caroline and our children Desmond and Annelise, and to my parents, sister, and family in New Brunswick.

INTRODUCTION

Ever since there have been missiles, people have tried to build missile defences. And ever since the Americans have tried to build missile defences, there have been Canadians wanting to help them.

When Prime Minister Paul Martin announced on February 24, 2005, that Canada would not join the latest iteration of the American missile shield, which was being proposed by President George W. Bush's administration, he brought to a close the first round of the debate on Bush's shield—but by no means the last round.

As an issue, missile defence did not follow Paul Martin's departure from Canadian politics when the Conservatives came to power in January 2006. Quite the contrary: Prime Minister Stephen Harper has expressed his willingness to revisit discussions with the United States on Canada's potential role in the shield. There is little doubt that a new round on missile defence will open in the near future.

By virtue of our position next to the United States, situated here between the lower forty-eight states and Russia, Canada has always been involved in America's ballistic missile-defence (BMD) schemes, and there have been many bouts of missile defence debates in Canada. These go right back to Prime Minister John Diefenbaker's reluctance to accept nuclear-armed Bomarc missiles in Canada and Lester B. Pearson's embrace of them in order to win the 1963 election.

Missile-defence programs developed by the United States have threatened to ensnare Canada many times. In 1972, the Anti-Ballistic Missile Treaty (ABM) between the United States and Russia prohibited most missile defences, but it never suffocated the desires of nuclear-weapons builders, planners, and strategists who were seeking a system that could neutralize the threat of an enemy's attack, giving the possessor of such a system an incredible advantage and freedom of action.

On March 23, 1983, U.S. president Ronald Reagan reignited the drive for missile defence when he announced the Strategic Defense Initiative, a program that would research and develop a fantastic array of ground-based (and space-based) weapons that could destroy Soviet missiles launched against the United States.

Just as in recent days, American allies were invited to participate in the program. Then, under Conservative prime minister Brian Mulroney, Canada declined. Eventually the program was scaled back, but remained active in one form or another despite the end of the Cold War. George Bush, Sr., and later Bill Clinton continued the research at a low level but kept the option open for a future president to re-establish the work in earnest.

President George W. Bush stoked the program by pledging to deploy a limited system during his first term in office. This would require withdrawal from the 1972 ABM treaty—which he announced on December 14, 2001. Under President Bush's plan, the military would deploy an initial system with limited capability, simultaneously developing and improving system components, thus testing the system as it was being deployed, piece by piece.

Bush's system would use satellites and ground-based radars to watch for enemy missile launches, especially from North Korea, which is viewed as the country most likely to develop the capacity to launch an attack on the United States at some time in the future. The system would additionally have the capability to shoot down an accidental launch of a few missiles from China or Russia.

Attempts to destroy the enemy missile would be made in each of the three phases of the missile's flight. During the earliest, or boost, phase, missiles deployed on land or aboard ships near the enemy's launching point would try to intercept the enemy missile in a collision when it was most vulnerable, before it entered outer space and the nuclear war-head or multiple warheads (perhaps decoys as well) separated from the missile's rocket booster. During the boost phase, a jumbo jet mounted with a laser (currently in development) would attempt to "zap" the enemy missile as it rose above the clouds towards outer space.

If these attempts to shoot down the missile failed, then radars would continue to track the warheads and decoys during their mid-course phase, as they travelled along their trajectory in a graceful arc through space towards their targets in the continental United States.

More interceptor missiles launched from sites in Alaska and California would fly into space and release self-propelled "kill vehi-cles," which could manoeuvre themselves through the vacuum of space into the anticipated path of the enemy warheads to destroy them in a seventeen-thousand-mile-per-hour collision, like a bullet hitting a bullet.

If the ground-based mid-course defence system failed, then a final attempt would be made to collide with the enemy warhead in its ter-minal phase as it re-entered the atmosphere in its final countdown to detonation above the target. Terminal-phase defences are still largely undefined, but could include smaller interceptor missiles such as the Patriot missiles used during the 1991 Gulf War against Iraq's SCUD missiles.

The system was controversial, as all missile-defence systems have been. Critics argued that, despite billions of dollars spent on research, the system was not ready for deployment. There were many critical components missing, and it could be easily fooled by decoys. It would also consume nearly $10 billion a year in reacting to a remote threat, while more likely threats by terrorists—such as a bomb delivered to the United States aboard a rusty freighter, rather than by an intercontinen-tal ballistic missile—were inadequately addressed.

Others feared the system would create distrust at best, and an arms race at worst, with Russia and China, for they would build more and improved missiles that could overcome any American defences simply as deterrents against the United States's nuclear arsenal of thousands of missiles.

Finally, future plans for the system included space-based missile inter-ceptors, which critics argued would broach the weaponization of space for the first time, possibly launching a whole new arms race in space weapons.

* * *

President Bush announced on December 17, 2002, that he had direct-ed Defense Secretary Donald Rumsfeld to field an initial set of missile defence capabilities. "We plan to begin operating these initial capabil-ities in 2004 and 2005, and they will include ground-based intercep-tors, sea-based interceptors, additional Patriot (PAC-3) units, and sen-sors based on land, at sea, and in space," President Bush said in a writ-ten statement.

This announcement at the end of 2002 that the United States had decided to go beyond research and testing, to actual deployment of a missile shield, started round one of the debate in Canada on George W. Bush's missile shield program. It lasted about two years, and ended on February 24, 2005, when Paul Martin declared that "Canada will not take part in the proposed ballistic missile defence system."

It is worth recalling here how that debate unfolded in Canada.

Within a month of Bush's announcement, Prime Minister Jean Chrétien agreed to initiate discussions to explore Canada's participa-tion in the U.S. ground-based, mid-course portion of the missile-defence system. When talks were officially announced in Parliament in May 2003, the expectation was that negotiations and a subsequent decision by Cabinet would be made quickly. Then-defence minister John McCallum optimistically predicted that they would be ready for a Cabinet decision "in a hundred days."

But there was no quick decision as McCallum had predicted, and the issue was handed to Paul Martin when he won the race to replace Chrétien as party leader and prime minister. Paul Martin made his preference for joining missile defence part of his leadership campaign, but he supported the Liberals' policy of opposing the weaponization of space. For his first Cabinet in December 2003 he selected as defence minister a fellow missile-defence supporter, David Pratt.

Defence Minister Pratt now oversaw the government's negotiations on missile defence and, along with foreign affairs minister, Bill Graham, led the campaign to win over public support for Canada's involvement in the U.S. program. But still, no decision was made to join before Paul Martin decided to call a federal election for June 2004.

Missile defence was an issue during the election, but anger over the "sponsorship scandal" cost the Liberals many seats. They were re-elected, but with only a minority government, outnumbered by the combined strength of the opposition parties.

The New Democratic Party and the Bloc Québécois opposed missile defence, and the Conservatives withheld their support until a final deal was presented to parliament to be voted upon. Despite the fact that the government could legally join the United States without such a vote, because of their minority position the Liberals were forced to agree to the demands of the Conservatives and other parties.

While missile-defence proponents in the media, business, and the military urged the government to join, citizen organizations, scientists, former diplomats, and even retired U.S. generals urged the government to say "no."

In August 2004, the government took a half-step towards joining by permitting missile warning and tracking information from the joint Canada–U.S. NORAD command to be used by the U.S.-only command that the Americans had decided would operate the missile defences. The government argued that the arrangement would preserve NORAD's role in continental defence, without representing a government decision to join missile defence outright.

Opposition to missile defence was growing amongst the public, and—more importantly for Paul Martin's minority government— within his caucus and his party as a whole. The Women's Caucus, the Quebec Caucus, and the Young Liberals voiced concern and proposed anti-missile-defence resolutions for the Liberal convention, which was to be held in March 2005. Oddly, having previously voiced support for missile defence, the prime minister left the job of promoting the system to his new defence minister Bill Graham.

The new parliament resumed in the fall, with the opposition parties pressing Paul Martin to reject missile defence and the defence and big-business lobbies—not to mention most of the media—urging him to join.

Within the divided Liberal caucus, an open confrontation erupted over the issue, and over U.S. relations generally, resulting in the prime minister expelling caucus member Carolyn Parrish. After this, the issue continued to dog the prime minister, and became a very sensitive topic for him and his minority government, which was no doubt quietly hoping that the November U.S. presidential election would provide them with some relief.

It was not to be. President Bush was re-elected that fall and, on his first official visit to Canada a few weeks later, Bush used his keynote speech in Halifax to say he hoped that Canada would join the U.S. ballistic-missile defence program. Martin responded angrily, and began to set conditions on Canada's potential participation. These included Canadian influence over the system and the assurance that Canada would provide no funding, no territory for missile interceptors, and no hand in the possible weaponization of space.

The year 2004 ended with several setbacks to the U.S. program: President Bush failed to fulfill his pledge, because the system was not declared operational, and in December the system's first test in two years failed. Two months later, the system failed again.

In Canada, public opinion continued to turn against Canada's participation, and a majority felt that it was an issue over which it would be worth going to an election. The Conservatives continued to withhold their support, despite the fact that, if they joined with pro-missiledefence Liberals, they had enough seats to pass a vote on a missiledefence deal.

In February 2005, Canadian ambassador-designate to the U.S., Frank McKenna, told reporters that Canada was already "part of" the U.S. shield, due to the previous summer's change to NORAD, which allowed missile-launch warning information to be shared with the U.S. command that ran the missile shield. Trying to weather the subsequent storm of controversy, the government denied a decision had been made, released its budget (which included large military-spending increases), and then, on February 24, finally announced that

Canada would "not take part in the proposed ballistic missile defence system."

* * *

That is the story as it will appear in the history books, but it's not the whole story. Behind the headlines was a David-and-Goliath struggle between those who wanted Canada to join missile defence and curry favour with the Bush administration and those who wanted Canada to maintain its long-held policy of opposition to missile defence and work towards nuclear disarmament and the prevention of an arms race in space. I probably don't need to tell you which side was carrying the slingshot.

This book will explain how a group of people worked together to shift public attitudes on missile defence, using the media and community-level organizing, and took advantage of the minority government to work with, among, and within all of the political parties to achieve their ultimate goal: to prevent Canada from joining the U.S. missile-defence system.

The Canadian Campaign to Oppose Missile Defence, as it was known among its participants, mounted a year-long campaign, using modest resources and the talents of a handful of citizen groups. This small campaign eventually prevailed over a pro–missile defence lobby that could draw upon the resources of the government and corporate backers. Despite the fact that practically every newspaper in the country supported missile defence editorially, the campaign managed to garner media attention through well-timed events and compelling emissaries, particularly from the United States.

This book is intended to provide another view of the missile-defence debate that gripped Canada for two years, from 2003 until early 2005. It's a view from inside the campaign that eventually moved Paul Martin from his belief that it was in Canada's interest to join missile defence to finally replying "no" to George W. Bush's invitation.

If you were among those who watched the political debate unfold, it will introduce you to the lesser-known players and events behind some of the evening television news broadcasts. If you are part of a cit-

izen group working on other issues, this book will share some of the
campaign's successful strategies and tactics, and some of the not-so
successful ones. I hope the lessons learned can help you to achieve victory.

1

FREE TRADE AND MISSILES

"The anticipation in the room is palpable," I thought as I took my seat in the swanky Laurier Room of the Fairmont Château Laurier Hotel. It was filled with mandarins from all the major federal government departments, who had come together to learn about the new political winds that were blowing through Ottawa.

It was early December 2003, and I was rather self-consciously joining a two-day conference entitled "New Directions: Managing the Canada–U.S. Relationship," which was being held only a stone's throw from Parliament Hill in downtown Ottawa. At a cost of $850 for each registrant, this event was not intended for low-level bureaucrats, and especially not for people like me working in non-governmental organizations who spend their days scratching nickels together and earnestly trying to get the government to "do the right thing." My organization, the Polaris Institute, and two other groups had to share the $850 registration fee so that we could have at least one person on the inside. That's why I was there.

That kind of entrance fee sends a signal that only the Ottawa elites should attend—and the message had been clearly received. A scan down the list of participants in the conference gave a sense of the room: the Associate Deputy Minister of Foreign Affairs and International Trade, the Secretary of the NAFTA Secretariat, the Director of the Canada Customs and Revenue Agency, the senior foreign policy

adviser for the Privy Council Office, the Vice President–Canada for
Boeing Corporation, the Assistant Director of the Treasury Board of
Canada Secretariat, the Director of Environment Canada, the President
and CEO of the Canadian Gas Association, and the President and CEO
of the Aerospace Industries Association of Canada.

The event was billed as an international forum on "Canada's new
strategy for dealing with today's top bilateral challenges: trade, trans-
portation, energy, the environment, immigration, defence, and security." It was organized by a little-known group called the Pacific Business
and Law Institute, but it had major backing from the Solicitor General
of Canada, the department of Critical Infrastructure Protection and
Emergency Preparedness, and the Canada Customs and Revenue
Agency.

All the few hundred seats were filled—and for good reasons. The
managers of the government machinery were preparing for new political leadership to arrive in Ottawa, with a new list of policy priorities.
By the end of the week Paul Martin, CEO and long-time finance minister, was set to move into the prime minister's residence at 24 Sussex
Drive.

In December 2003 Paul Martin was sailing into the PM's office on a
tidal wave of support. It was during this period that Martin received his
highest public-approval rating ever. Pundits were predicting that
Martin's immense popularity could sweep the next election, knocking
the Bloc Québécois out in Quebec, gobbling up Conservative seats in
the West, and possibly reducing the NDP to a mere handful of seats—
if any at all. The Martin machine seemed unstoppable.

In Ottawa, many of the lobbyists and think-tanks that had worked
behind the scenes with the Martin camp for years were moving into
position, ready to take power. The Ottawa political elites were adjust-
ing to the new leadership, and this conference, like many others on
similar topics held during this period, were designed to entrench the
Martin agenda. As if to underline this, as the conference opened, there,
taking the stage as the conference co-chair, was one of the most successful of Ottawa's back-room operators, and the face of "corporate
Canada," Tom d'Aquino.

D'Aquino's biography in the conference program referred to him as a lawyer, entrepreneur, and strategist. But he was best known as the head of the Business Council on National Issues (BCNI)—the chief corporate lobby group that had worked with the government of Brian Mulroney to bring in the first Free Trade Agreement with the United States in 1989. In 2001, the old BCNI was rebranded as the Canadian Council of Chief Executives. In the conference kit, the CCCE was said to be composed of 150 chief executive officers and was described as the senior voice of Canadian business on public-policy issues in Canada, the United States, and internationally.

D'Aquino wasted no time in making his point: that managing the Canada–U.S. relationship requires accepting that

> Global conflict is no longer limited to the kind of armies, nor does it remain the exclusive domain of nations . . . this fact was driven home brutally by the terrorist attacks of September 11, 2001. The way that we and other countries respond to the relentless threat of terrorism and rogue states has vital implications for global economic growth, just as it does for Canada's future—both as a trade-dependent economy and as an immigration-based society.

D'Aquino has been behind all the major corporate initiatives in Canada for the past twenty-five years: not just the Free Trade Agreement, but later the North American Free Trade Agreement (NAFTA), federal spending cuts to reduce the deficit, promotion of the privatization of government services, promotion of global trade talks at the World Trade Organization, and the Free Trade Area of the Americas. His influence has twisted its way through Liberal and Conservative governments alike.

But interestingly, he has focused most recently on linking free trade with increased military and security integration—or co-operation, as he would put it—with the United States. He made his case from the conference podium:

For Canada, and for the world as a whole, economic security and physical security have become inseparable. Now while these dual challenges are global, there is no escaping the fact that for Canada, our relationship with the United States—what I call Rome on the Potomac—will be pivotal to any strategy that we may adopt. The United States is at once a neighbour, sharing a border that stretches thousands of kilometres, a trading partner that accounts for the vast majority of our imports and exports, our closest military ally, and the world's dominant superpower.

After going through the many ways terrorism can have an impact on free trade, d'Aquino came directly to the point, leaning into the microphone:

The signing of the Free Trade Agreement in 1988 marked a turning point in Canada's economic strategy that, I believe, has paid huge dividends. Now we must integrate our plans for achieving economic advantage within North America with a strategy for ensuring the security both of our own borders, and of the continent as a whole.

As I listened, it dawned on me that what he was describing was no less than "Fortress North America." That's not a term that he would use, but in essence he was saying that the integration of the Canadian economy with the U.S. economy as a result of free trade now required a new phase of military and security integration. The possible implications of this kind of integration are astounding: the adoption of U.S. rules for our immigration policies, sharing information on Canadians with the CIA and the FBI, and equipping our military with the types of weapons used by the United States, such as the most advanced and lethal laser-guided bombs.

The linking of free trade with security would form the basis for a powerful lobby in Canada—in fact it yoked together the interests of both the "corporate lobby," which d'Aquino represented, and the

small-yet-influential "defence lobby." Both groups sought greater continental security, increases in military spending, and participation in
U.S.-led wars abroad—including the Bush administration's global War
on Terrorism.

For the defence lobby, the closest possible relationship with the
Pentagon—whether through alliances such as NATO and NORAD or
participation in U.S.-led wars such as those in the Persian Gulf and the
former Yugoslavia—has always been the goal. Along with that has
come an insatiable demand for more military spending, more troops,
and more weaponry.

The corporate lobby, which has never until now had much reason to
focus on defence and foreign policy, suddenly realized that, after
September 11, 2001, dealing with the Bush administration meant that
the issues of trade and security would be brought together. In fact, in
the words of then-U.S. ambassador to Canada, Paul Cellucci, in the
United States "security trumps trade."

A printout of a presentation made by Tom d'Aquino back in January
2003 to his group's board of directors, composed of Bay Street CEOs,
was circulating around the room. It was entitled "Security and
Prosperity: The Dynamics of a New Canada–United States Partnership
in North America."

The presentation generally followed the same line as the speech I
was listening to, so I flipped through it to the section entitled "The
Strategy—Part IV: Sharing in Continental and Global Security." It read:

> The preoccupation of the United States with national security
> is total. . . . We must enhance the interoperability of Canadian
> and United States armed forces on land, at sea, and in the air,
> including Canadian participation in a continental anti-ballis-
> tic missile system.

That's why our campaign to prevent Canada from joining the U.S.
missile-defence system was squared-off against a powerful array of missile-defence proponents. The corporate lobby, and the defence lobby
had seized on Canada's joining the Bush administration's pet military

project as the greatest single act that could win favour in the United States—especially after Canada had decided not to join the so-called coalition of the willing in the U.S.-led invasion of Iraq.

Missile defence was considered a priority military system by the Bush administration, consistently winning the highest spending increases of any program. True believers in the technology, Republican Party hawks have looked to missile defence as if to the Holy Grail.

Maybe if we joined them, Canadian proponents would argue, the United States would be willing to resolve a growing list of trade disputes with Canada. Canadian exporters were losing billions of dollars because of U.S. rules that kept Canadian cattle out of the United States and exacted crippling duties on Canadian softwood lumber exports. As the U.S. government ignored one unfavourable trade ruling after another from the WTO and NAFTA dispute panels, it was becoming clear to Canadians that NAFTA was unravelling at the hands of the protectionist U.S. Congress and the hawkish Bush administration.

This is why, during so much of the public debate, proponents for missile defence tossed out statistics on how much trade crossed the border every day, rather than on the number of missiles poised to attack Canada. Examining their argument, I concluded that the missile-defence issue was not about protecting Canada at all—it was about salvaging NAFTA.

* * *

Everyone remembers where they were and what they were doing that bright and sunny fall day that was September 11, 2001. Probably only a few people, though, immediately realized how profoundly everything would change following the destruction of the twin New York towers by those hijacked airliners.

I was just arriving at my downtown Ottawa office, where I was the issues campaign coordinator for Canada's largest citizen organization, the Council of Canadians. Council is headed by one of the country's most respected social activists, Maude Barlow, someone who taught me a great deal about the need to defend traditional Canadian values against those who put the bottom line before all else.

We had spent the last few weeks preparing for the next big meeting of the World Trade Organization, which was scheduled for November in the tiny Persian Gulf state of Qatar. The Council of Canadians was a leading organization in the flourishing and successful anti-corporate-globalization movement that was sweeping the world at the time.

As we watched the footage of the towers collapsing and soot-covered businessmen running for their lives down Wall Street, the impact of the terrorist attacks began to sink in. Watching it all unfold, John Urquhart, our executive director and someone with a good sense of the political moment, said, "Corporate America will now be seen as a victim."

The United States had been sucker-punched. No doubt about it, these terrorist strikes would politically strengthen the Bush administration and proponents of globalization.

In the weeks, months, and even years that followed September 11, 2001, the anti-corporate-globalization movement was undeniably in a "funk." The terrorist attacks divided our coalitions of social-justice activists, anti-poverty groups, development organizations, environmentalists, and trade unionists. The massive protests against globalization that had been organized at the World Trade Organization talks in Seattle in 1999, Washington in 2000, and Quebec City in 2001 had been very effective at pressing our demands, but tensions between more mainstream organizations and the typically black-clad younger activists who wanted to take direct action were growing, especially after Quebec City.

International alliances, especially those involving colleagues in the United States, were strained as well. The U.S. labour movement had come out in favour of the invasion of Afghanistan in response to the terrorist attacks, and that pressure not to oppose the president or the war was being felt throughout progressive networks in the United States.

For some, the confusion that erupted within the anti-corporate-globalization movement stemmed from disagreement over tactics. To many mainstream organizations, images of groups of people or even a single person throwing rocks at the police or at a storefront would be unacceptable to the public after all the violence in New York, which was being replayed over and over again on television.

Others argued that the destruction of the terrorist attacks in New York had to be compared to the daily hunger of millions of people around the world. They pointed out that a broken window at a Starbucks was not as important as children starving to death because of World Bank and IMF strict financial rules imposed on developing countries. They wanted the protests to continue.

But in my view this debate missed a more important fact: that the anti-corporate-globalization movement, in its analysis of international debt, trade, and globalization, was unable to explain the role of military power in globalization. This blind spot was a concern for me personally, because I had spent the last decade working in the anti-corporate-globalization movement at the Council of Canadians and in the peace movement through a Vancouver organization called End the Arms Race.

So, in 2002 my good friend and respected ally Alice Slater of the Global Action Resource Center (GRACE) in New York, provided me with a three-year grant to work on a project that would make the links between globalization and militarism. Taking on this work didn't fit with my role at the Council of Canadians, so I moved to the Polaris Institute, which is headed by Maude Barlow's long-time colleague Tony Clarke.

Tony has committed many years to making the world a better place for everyone, and has a deep understanding of myriad issues and of how people can work through them to create a just society. The two of us set about establishing a new project at the Polaris Institute that would work with the public, social movements, policy-makers, and journalists.

It was difficult, but we had some success helping groups understand how militarism protected the inherent inequality within the global system to the benefit of rich nations, and how globalization sowed the seeds of conflict everywhere. Ultimately we found that the best way to educate people was to engage them in specific issues that could serve as illustrations of the deeper forces at play.

Missile defence, like few other issues, was an obvious connection point for people: they could understand how the pressure to accept U.S.

leadership at the expense of Canada's own traditional values of peace and multilateralism would fundamentally undermine our sovereignty—and our democracy. In the United States missile defence was driven by Cold War ideology and the "triumphalism" that came out of winning the Cold War, and was supported by the major arms-manufacturing conglomerates of Boeing, Lockheed Martin, and Raytheon, which would win the lion's share of billions in contracts. In Canada, big business didn't care much about shooting down missiles, but they were willing to learn to care about it because Bush cared about it, and so corporate Canada took up the torch for missile defence.

Ironically, as our social movement struggled to make the connections between global free enterprise—capitalism, if you will—and the spread of military power, the link was abundantly clear to the Bush administration and their allies among big business in Canada. The CEOs understood perfectly well that their economic security was linked to military security, and that's why they led the charge to appease George W. Bush in any way possible, despite what "ordinary" Canadians might feel. That is why, as a result of their failure to convince Prime Minister Jean Chrétien to join the U.S.-led invasion of Iraq, the next obvious goal for the corporate leaders was to convince Paul Martin to join Bush's missile-defence system.

* * *

My favourite part of Michael Moore's movie *Fahrenheit 9/11* is the footage of George W. Bush at the moment he learns that the second World Trade Tower has been hit by a hijacked aircraft. He is sitting in a classroom of school children, listening to the teacher read a children's book called *My Pet Goat*, when his assistant leans close to the his ear and reportedly whispers, "America is under attack."

Bush sits in a kind of stunned, expressionless silence for what seems like a very long time—about five minutes, in fact. Moore, in his famous comedic fashion, adds his own voice-over, suggesting what Bush may have been thinking as he sat listening to *My Pet Goat*: "Oh no, who's screwed me now? . . . I bet it was those Saudis . . . Maybe I shouldn't have taken so many naps and vacations . . . "

But as we now know from a report by the Associated Press, Bush wasted little time in seizing the political opportunity that had been handed to him. Twelve hours later, in a cramped nuclear bunker deep below the White House, Bush gathered his national-security team around the table and declared, "This is our time."

President Bush had just finished his famous televised address on the day of the attacks, in which he said, "We will make no distinction between the terrorists who committed these acts and those who harbour them," laying the first stone in the road that would lead to a rewriting of U.S. national-security policy.

According to Richard A. Clarke, President Clinton's "terrorism czar" and key adviser in the hunt for Osama bin Laden, when the Bush administration took office they demonstrated little interest in preventing an al-Qaeda attack on the United States, and, as Clarke described it, were blinded by an "ideological obsession" with invading Iraq and building a missile-defence system. In fact, according to Clarke, the attacks of September 11, 2001, prevented National Security Adviser Condoleezza Rice from giving a speech that day that would have promoted missile defence, and would not have mentioned bin Laden or al-Qaeda at all.

Bush had already stated his intention to build a missile-defence system, even before the terrorist attacks. However, the many plans of Bush and his administration, such as Defense Secretary Donald Rumsfeld's agenda to reform the U.S. military's Cold War conceptualization of fighting a war by the adoption of more lethal, rapid, and high-tech technologies, loosely described as "the Revolution in Military Affairs," were meeting resistance from the military.

As rumour has it, even Ronald Reagan's original vision of the Strategic Defense Initiative was eventually derailed by foot-dragging by the military itself. As the incredible cost of building such a system became apparent, generals who were seeking to protect the budgets for their pet projects, such as new aircraft or warships, saw missile defence as a threat.

But the wave of political momentum created by September 11, 2001, swept all resistance aside and, as George W. Bush told his team on that day, this was the time to move forward their agenda on Iraq and on missile defence. This was indeed their time.

* * *

An oft-repeated quote amongst left-wing organizations is one made by anthropologist Margaret Mead. It can be found on posters, on T-shirts, in e-mails, and in PowerPoint presentations. I once had a coffee cup with her quote emblazoned on the side: "Never doubt that a small group of thoughtful, committed people can change the world. Indeed, it is the only thing that ever has."

Ironically, this little inspirational saying could apply equally to a few people in Washington, D.C. who have been diehard proponents of missile defence for decades—and these people never give up.

My first encounter with one of the missile-defence true believers was on the CBC Newsworld television program "counterSpin." It was a terrific program, and its host Avi Lewis, and later others, took a fair but unabashedly progressive position on all kinds of issues. It was a debate-format program between two duos who held opposing points of view.

I appeared on the program a few times over its successful six-year run, but on one occasion I was put up against Frank Gaffney, Jr., live from Washington, D.C. Frank Gaffney, I have been told, was considered too radically right wing even for the Bush administration, so he was never given a post, and it must have been terribly disappointing for him to miss guiding into reality his life-long dream—a missile-defence system.

In 1988, Gaffney had founded his own group, called the Center for Security Policy, whose motto is "Promoting Peace through Strength." During the Reagan administration he worked as assistant secretary of defense and deputy assistant secretary of defense for Richard Perle, a peripheral member of the current Bush administration, who is often described as "the Prince of Darkness" because of his ultra-hawkish views and brooding demeanour.

If you are watching a television program like *CounterSpin*, you see the host in the studio, maybe a few guests seated around a table, and then a few more on a big TV screen in the background, calling in from Washington or some other location. It all looks perfectly normal, but the truth is that the guests who are not in the studio are undergoing the strange experience of being bound up in wires in a dark room, with the whole world watching their every flinch and scratch. As a guest you're on the air live, straining to hear the host and the other guests through the squawky little thing in your ear while staring down the black, unblinking lens of the camera. It's no wonder many participants on these programs look like deer in the headlights.

Frank Gaffney, however, was an old hand at TV talk shows. In fact, he had become a sort of one-man media machine, promoting missile defence to anyone who would put a microphone in front of him. To the surprise of some people, no doubt, Frank Gaffney has no horns growing out of his head. In fact, he has that U.S. old-school playful charm that I have found so many American military men to possess. It makes them immediately approachable and, frankly, difficult to debate, because even while they're explaining why we should blow up someone else's country, they're being just so darn likeable.

When I appeared on *CounterSpin* with Frank Gaffney, Avi had turned over the hosting of the program to the very capable Carol Off. In addition to Gaffney, University of Manitoba professor James Fergusson was on the program to play along with Frank Gaffney, former Canadian former Canadian Foreign Affairs Minister Lloyd Axworthy, and I.

Carol said, "Jim I want you to start off. Can you tell us, will this missile-defence system work?"

"Well I think we should be optimistic," replied Jim. "We should go back to 1961. When John Kennedy announced that the United States would go to the moon there were a lot of skeptics who said it couldn't be done—and it was done . . . at the end of the day I think the technology will mature, the real issue is: how effective does it have to be, to be useful?"

Next it was my turn. "Steven Staples, how confident are you?" asked Carol.

"Well I'm not confident at all," I said. "Because I think people are being sold a bill of goods that this is going to work. This is rocket science—and I go to the scientists myself to see what they're saying. The Union of Concerned Scientists issued their independent report earlier this year that said the technology is barely out of the testing phase, it's barely out of the laboratory. There is a real danger that Americans may put this system up and think that they're defended when they really aren't."

"Frank Gaffney?"

"Needless to say, I disagree," he said. "I think that Jim has it about right, this is a program that is evolving. I am amused by this statement that the American people will wrongly assume they have a missile defence. The American people have wrongly assumed they had a missile defence for years. This is a very common response in public-opinion polling that I, among others, did for decades. The reality is that we are better off having an even partially effective system."

* * *

At the time of the September 11, 2001, attacks, the Canadian Department of National Defence's policy group was going to press with its global security survey, *Strategic Assessment 2001*. Just as we had to "stop the presses" at the Council of Canadians, these military analysts must have had to stop the publication of their strategic assessment in light of the terrorist attacks.

The analysts quickly wrote a two-page assessment of the global changes that the terrorist attacks against the U.S. would precipitate, and attached it to the end of the main report as an "epilogue." The assessment was chilling and predicted the dramatic global military buildup, large-scale conventional military operations, and the abandonment of international law in favour of achieving military objectives.

The DND analysts concluded that transnational terrorism would be regarded as the primary threat to international security, and that "the balance between the notion of 'human security' and traditional concepts of security will likely shift in the direction of defending national territory and populations and away from championing poverty eradication and human rights." The result would be that "Previous concerns

to avoid combat casualties in military operations and to minimize col-
lateral damage will be of less importance than achieving military
objectives."

Further, DND saw that international law would be cast aside in the
search for terrorists, "The standards of proof for complicity in or
responsibility for terrorist attacks before undertaking counter-terrorist
actions will likely be relaxed in favour of results."

DND analysts predicted that the United States would move ahead
on missile defence. "Americans' heightened sense of territorial vulner-
ability will intensify homeland defence initiatives, including those
relating to ballistic missile defence," the report said.

But perhaps most prescient were the defence analysts' understanding
of the expectations that the Bush administration would place on allies
such as Canada. "The international system will be re-ordered into allies
or enemies in the fight against terror," wrote the analysts. "Countries
that try to adopt a neutral stance will find themselves under pressure
to take sides. Traditional U.S. allies will find that calls for military,
diplomatic and other support from Washington will be regarded as a
test of their loyalty."

* * *

Shortly after President Bush said to his cabinet "This is our time," and
while war plans were being laid for the attack on Afghanistan, he used
the occasion of his September 20, 2001, speech to the special Joint
Session of Congress to issue his challenge to governments around the
world: "Every nation, in every region, now has a decision to make.
Either you are with us, or you are with the terrorists."

The stark choice put before old enemies and allies alike, including
Canada, made it clear that the United States expected not just support
for, but active participation in, the looming War on Terrorism.

But despite the challenge, and corporate Canada's exhortations to
join the U.S.-led "coalition of the willing" for the attack on Iraq in the
same way that Canada had already joined the invasion of Afghanistan,
Prime Minister Chrétien announced on March 17, 2003, that Canada
would not join the war.

Days later, the U.S. ambassador to Canada, Paul Cellucci, used a speech to the Economic Club of Toronto to express his country's displeasure with the Chrétien government's decision. "There is a lot of disappointment in Washington and a lot of people are upset," said Ambassador Cellucci.

His speech to the Canadian corporate elite kicked off a series of public engagements and media appearances, which the ambassador used to lambaste the Chrétien government. Rumour was that Cellucci got his instructions for the very public display of displeasure directly from the White House, even from the president personally.

"Security will trump trade," said Ambassador Cellucci, raising the spectre of increased frustrations of trade at the border. It was a carefully crafted message, designed to stir up resistance to the Chrétien government and to energize pro-U.S. elements of the Canadian body politic. He appealed to the business class, the Canadian Alliance Party, the Progressive Conservative Party, conservative elements of the Liberal Party, and especially the military.

The U.S. government's interference in the Canadian political debate split the Chrétien Liberals. Some members could barely contain their anger over the prime minister's decision to not join the war. Others, including some Cabinet members, wanted to send Cellucci packing back to Washington. But with polls showing a majority of Canadians opposed to the war, especially in Quebec, the prime minister chose to side with average people on Main Street instead of the corporate CEOs and bankers of Bay Street.

Concern about the impact that new U.S. security measures at the border would have on Canadian access to the American market remained a major issue for Canadian business in the wake of September 11, 2001. False reports that the terrorist hijackers came from Canada stoked unwarranted fears in the United States that the long, undefended border between the two countries was a security risk.

The fact that the Canada–U.S. border was closed by American officials during those September days of crisis, disrupting the NAFTA-integrated economies, promoted a series of discussions between the two governments to help facilitate trade in a more security-conscious environment. Canadian business urged the government to satisfy U.S. security concerns to avoid onerous and profit-damaging security measures at the border.

Bill Dymond, a former Canadian trade negotiator and current director of a free-trade think-tank at Carleton University, argued,

> Just as the NAFTA and the WTO could not prevent the closure of the border in September 2001, so they are unable to move beyond trade rules and deal with security, immigration and cooperation on geopolitical issues which are becoming increasingly the touchstone of U.S. foreign policy, including trade policy.

Others agreed. "NAFTA has largely outlived its usefulness," wrote Wendy Dobson of the corporate-funded C.D. Howe Institute in the *Globe and Mail*. "Canadian concerns about economic security must be linked with U.S. domestic priorities to attract U.S. notice. And homeland security is the single overriding U.S. goal. What's needed is a strategic framework that links security and defence with economic goals."

* * *

Whether anyone in the room at that conference in the Château Laurier in December 2003 actually understood what Tom d'Aquino was talking about in his long-winded, rather convoluted way is open for debate. But everyone's ears perked up for the next speaker, U.S. ambassador Paul Cellucci.

Cellucci's tone was much lighter than during that speech eight months earlier in Toronto, and he avoided mentioning the U.S.'s sore feelings about Canada staying out of Iraq. As he told the audience,

> I think I can tell you and report to you that the Canada–U.S. relationship is in very good shape. We have been moving forward and I think it is in each of our nation's interests, Canada and the United States, to keep it moving forward. That's what we very much expect will happen when the new [Martin] government comes in, in just two days.

But the message about the United States's desire for increased military co-operation between Canada and the United States remained. The crucial difference was that the focus had shifted from the war in Iraq to a new project: missile defence.

> Obviously for us in the United States of America, our top priority remains the defeat of international terrorism. And we work very closely with the Canadian military, with Canadian intelligence and the law enforcement community on this goal. In just the past year or so we've reached an agreement with the Canadian military for the Bi-National Planning Group out at NORTHCOM, which is our new command out at Colorado Springs. These military people are working together on the defence of North America—the land, the sea, in addition to the air defence where we've had a joint command for over 40 years: NORAD, the North American Aerospace Defence Command.

> We are very close, I would say we've had some good negotiations, and I'm optimistic that we will soon have agreement in principle on Canadian participation in missile defence. We're still discussing that. We think it is a logical extension of NORAD—this early warning system, NORAD—so that we can work together to protect our territory here in the northern part of this continent.

Cellucci seemed to have a lot of friends in the room. As he swept his way from the stage to the doors at the back of the room, he handed out waves, smiles, and nods to many folks in the audience. The only time it seemed that he actually stopped to shake anybody's hand was for a man across the aisle from me. Cellucci seemed to be honestly interested in saying hello to this guy.

Later, I got a closer look at Cellucci's chum and realized from his name tag that he worked for the notorious American public-relations firm Hill and Knowlten. That's the firm widely credited with helping

George Bush, Sr., win popular support for the first Gulf War back in
1991. I wondered if Hill and Knowlten had taken on any new contracts
lately that might involve a continental missile shield.

* * *

After two days of panels on security, defence, immigration, border
security, electricity, water, and NAFTA, it was time for the conference to
be brought to a conclusion. The task was left to the co-chairs of the
event, two men who did not always see eye to eye on the issues. In
addition to Tom d'Aquino, the organizers of the conference had enlist-
ed the Right Honourable Herb Grey, Jean Chrétien's deputy prime
minister and a long-time member of parliament, who had served as a
cabinet minister in many departments over the years.

The final moments of the conference were very revealing, because
the organizers had asked the two men to give their own visions to the
audience on "Integration, Security and Sovereignty: A Vision for
Canada's Future in North America."

Tom d'Aquino used his closing comments to tell a story, about himself and George Bush, Sr., that he felt "would give us hope." He began,

> In March of 1983, my organization [the BCNI] hosted then-
> Vice President George Bush. We met at the Château [Laurier]
> and had close to ninety minutes, and when we tried to sell the
> Vice President on the idea of a free-trade agreement his
> response was "What's in it for us?" And the response was, "A
> market, Mr. Vice President, the size of California." He looked
> up at the ceiling and said, "Gee, I never thought about that,"
> turned to [his assistant] and said, "Let's do some serious work
> on this issue."

> Let's go fast forward. This August, I had the great pleasure of
> being part of a fishing party with George Bush, Sr., now retired,
> a great fly fisherman, and we were up in northeastern Labrador.
> We had three and a half days—a lot of time to talk—and I
> talked about this issue. And again his question was, "Well

what's in it for us right now?" Answer: "At a time when the world is dramatically changed, at a time when North America faces a certainty of further terrorist attacks, and we are all so, so concerned about security—it offers us an opportunity to create together an island of prosperity and security among people who are genuinely friends and who have so, so much in common." And then he said, "Well I can get that and I'm sure that other people can get it too."

So I am very, very hopeful that we will see a change. And if anyone says "impossible" then just say, "September 11, to wit," that's what is going to make the difference.

It was clear that Herb Grey did not feel the same enthusiasm for such further integration of North America as did Tom d'Aquino. His final presentation was a tactful, rigorous, and poetic dismantling of much of d'Aquino's argument for deeper integration with the United States. In closing, Herb Grey quoted the thousand-year-old text of the Jewish sage Rabbi Hillel:

"If I am not for myself, who will be for me? If I am for myself alone, what am I? If not now, when?" So our vision, broadly defined, I submit, must involve being effective stewards now and in the future for ourselves and for our grandchildren, of that great and wonderful mass of land and waters that we call Canada. After all, if we are not for ourselves, who will be for us?

2

PAUL MARTIN FALLS FOR STAR WARS

For the average Canadian, it was never clear whether Paul Martin thought that Canada should have joined George W. Bush's "coalition of the willing" in the invasion of Iraq. At the time it was Jean Chrétien's call. Paul Martin was still preparing his leadership campaign to succeed Chrétien as head of the party.

When asked later whether he supported Jean Chrétien's anti-invasion position, Paul Martin always provided a response along the lines of "The government has made a decision and I support the government." This is not exactly a ringing endorsement of the decision not to join the invasion. In fact, it's the kind of response usually made by someone who does not support a decision, but will not break with the party line.

During his run for the leadership, Paul Martin was faulted for making vague statements, dodging questions, and sticking to rhetorical flourishes rather than providing policy specifics. Whether it was in the areas of foreign policy or health care, Martin's leadership opponents John Manley and Sheila Copps frequently criticized Martin for his indecisiveness on key issues facing Canada.

But on one issue Paul Martin had had a clear position: missile defence. On April 27, 2003, during an interview on CTV's Sunday-afternoon political program *Question Period*, Martin had said, "If there are going to be missiles that are going off and they're going to be going off in Canadian airspace whether we want it or not, no, that's not acceptable. I think that we want to be at the table."

Question Period co-host John Ibbitson asked Martin whether that meant Canada should join the U.S. missile plan. "So that's a yes? We should join?" asked Ibbitson.

"Well, I don't see why we would walk away from the opportunity to protect the northern half and have a say over what happens in our airspace," Martin replied. "I think we are essentially responsible for security on the North American continent," he went on, "and we do not want to be in a position where the United States feels that they have to come up here if they are going to protect their northern border."

Paul Martin's public endorsement of missile defence was an important victory for business groups such as the Canadian Council of Chief Executives and others who were pushing for Canada to join the American missile shield. As mentioned, to them, giving in to the United States on missile defence would help erase any hard feelings in Washington over Canada's refusal to join the invasion of Iraq. To business leaders, satisfying the Bush administration's near-total preoccupation with military and national security issues would open the door to improved Canada–U.S. relations generally, especially when it came to dealing with trade.

This was the thrust of a campaign by Tom d'Aquino's Canadian Council of Chief Executives (CCCE), which they called the Security and Prosperity Initiative. The campaign had been launched in January 2003 at a closed-door meeting in Toronto before an audience of some of Canada's wealthiest and most powerful CEOs.

"CEOs Urging Stronger Ties to U.S.: Group to Tout Opening Border, Beefing Up Military," proclaimed the headline in the *Globe and Mail*'s business section. The article quoted Tom d'Aquino as saying he had received "a very strong positive reaction from the [CCCE] members," which the *Globe* described as "a prestigious group of 150 leading chief executive officers."

The article reported that the CCCE stopped short of recommending a single large military for North America, but that d'Aquino said, "The U.S. preoccupation with security makes this a good time to bring in a perimeter defence network. Canadian interests would be protected should the United States shut down the border with Canada." It was clear from CCCE documents that building a North American security perimeter obviously included Canada joining the U.S. missile-defence system.

But CEOs weren't the only people who attended the CCCE's campaign launch. Paul Martin was there too, and he gave a speech that endorsed the CCCE's vision of increased security co-operation between Canada and the United States. "Clearly we're going to be looking for a great deal of co-operation between our two countries in terms of what they call homeland security and what we call national security, and obviously, given the events—international terrorism—that's something that we both want," the *Globe and Mail* reported Paul Martin as saying in his speech to the CEOs.

Martin's endorsement of big-business views, and his eventual public support of missile defence three months after meeting with Tom d'Aquino's group of CEOs, won him the corporations' support in his 2003 leadership campaign.

Later that summer, the influential Canadian Chamber of Commerce backed Paul Martin in his bid to become Liberal Party leader, specifically citing his support on missile defence. The business group, which represents 350 chambers of commerce across Canada, gave Martin a glowing endorsement in a report card on the leadership hopefuls.

"In terms of his very strong orientation of sound fiscal policy, he gets high marks, and he also gets high marks on Canada–U.S. issues, which I think are top two issues," the Chamber's president, Nancy Hughes Anthony, told the *Globe and Mail*. The Chamber "supports his view that Canada be part of the U.S. missile-defence strategy," reported the *Globe*.

Big-business support for Paul Martin made his eventual about-face on missile defence all the more dramatic. How did this resolute proponent of military co-operation become the man who had to tell George W. Bush that Canada would not join the U.S. missile-defence system, Bush's centrepiece of homeland security? The answer seems to be that, from time to time, the legitimacy of public opinion can override the influence of special interests. That is certainly what happened on missile defence.

* * *

A seismic shift took place in the Liberal government's attitude toward U.S. plans on missile defence in late December 2002. The government switched from its traditional position which was skeptical of missile defence to being open to starting talks on joining the U.S. system. Did the Ghost of Missile Defence visit the Liberal caucus that year to frighten them into believing in the magical system?

The Liberal's original position against missile defence apparently had been largely the result of former foreign-affairs minister Lloyd Axworthy's firm opposition to the project. Axworthy, a staunch advocate of multilateralism and champion of "soft power" diplomacy, had strengthened the Liberals' reluctance to engage the United States over Canada's potential involvement in missile defence.

However, Lloyd Axworthy's retirement from politics in 2000 left the door open for the Liberals to shift their position. Alarm bells should have started ringing when Canada responded weakly to the United States's withdrawal from its Anti-Ballistic Missile Treaty with Russia in order to build the missile-defence system. On December 13, 2001, President Bush said of the ABM Treaty: "It hinders our ability to develop ways to protect our people from future terrorist or rogue states from missile attacks. I cannot and will not allow the U.S. to remain in a treaty that prevents us from developing effective defences."

The Canadian government's response was the political equivalent of a shrug of the shoulders. This indifferent reaction was in stark contrast to previous government statements that described the treaty as the cornerstone of international efforts for nuclear disarmament. The writing was on the wall for a Canadian government shift in opinion in favour of missile defence.

This was the first time that the United States had withdrawn from a major treaty, and the Bush administration had isolated the country in the international community by taking such a unilateral and potentially destabilizing step. Many allies felt that engagement in the missile defence system risked chilling international relations with Russia and China, or could spark an arms race in space. In response to this international concern, the Bush administration began a campaign to win political support for the missile-defence scheme from its allies in Europe, Asia, and, of course, Canada.

In the summer of 2002, the respected U.S. defence-industry magazine *Defense News* revealed that the Pentagon had a plan to use military contracts to help win over reluctant governments. With an annual budget of nearly $10 billion a year, the Missile Defense Agency had a lot of money to spread around internationally, even though U.S. corporations were perfectly capable of building the system on their own.

Defense News reported that the Missile Defense Agency wanted to "lure foreign firms with U.S. military dollars and hope the contractors sway their governments to get on board." The theory was that corporate lobbies could push governments to join the system, increasing the possibility of plum contracts for corporations and jobs for voters who would support the ruling party.

In programs such as this where the military system was being built by the United States, foreign government support was essential for that foreign country's corporations to be considered trustworthy partners by the Pentagon, for they would be privy to U.S. technology.

That year Boeing, the lead contractor for U.S. continental missile defence, began negotiating co-production contracts with foreign defence companies. By October it had gotten around to Canada, and announced that it had signed a deal with Montreal-based CAE Inc. for modelling and simulation services for missile defence.

The value of the contract was never disclosed, but it was patently obvious that the contract was designed to inspire a corporate lobby in Canada to promote missile defence. CAE had no technology that wasn't already available in the United States, but it was the country's largest Canadian-owned defence contractor.

CAE was a wise choice by Boeing to gain political leverage over Ottawa, since at the time CAE's CEO was one of the best-connected people in Canada, Derek H. Burney. Burney was Brian Mulroney's former chief of staff, and, working with Tom d'Aquino as his private-sector ally, he had been the chief architect of the Canada–U.S. free trade agreement.

Burney later went on to become Canadian ambassador to the United States, building even more relationships in Washington. But in 2002, as head of CAE, he led Canada's largest defence corporation and sat on the boards of the Aerospace Industries Association of Canada and the Canadian Council of Chief Executives.

In December 2002, President Bush ordered the Pentagon to begin deployment of the missile-defence system with about a dozen interceptor missile stations in Alaska and California. The system was to be made operational in the fall of 2004. In Ottawa, it was felt that this deployment date served as a deadline for a Canadian decision on whether or not to join missile defence. The clock was ticking.

* * *

In January 2003, at about the same time the Canadian Council of Chief Executives was laying out its blueprint for greater integration with the United States, and calling on Ottawa to join missile defence, Defence Minister John McCallum was speaking to U.S. Secretary of Defense Donald Rumsfeld about Canada's potential role in the program. Defence Minister McCallum sent DND officials to Washington to "explore possible Canadian involvement in ballistic missile defence."

According to the Department of Foreign Affairs, the talks were indeed prompted by President Bush's December 2002 order to the Pentagon to deploy a missile defence system by the fall of 2004. "[This] is clearly a new and significant development. We will be seeking information from U.S. officials on a range of issues related to this decision," Canadian foreign affairs spokesperson Kimberly Phillips told Reuters.

In January 2003, Bill Graham said he had doubts about the system. Graham had been promoted from the chair of the Commons Foreign Affairs Committee to minister of foreign affairs. "We have questions about missile defence's potential impact on strategic stability, arms control, disarmament and the non-weaponization of space," said Phillips.

But Graham was surrounded by department officials who wanted Canada to join missile defence. One unnamed military source told Reuters, "Both the foreign and defence ministries feel it's in their interest to go ahead and take a hard look at this because the ball is rolling and it's probably to Canada's benefit—if it is going to participate—to be in there sooner rather than later."

The announcement of the exploratory meetings in 2003 between Canadian and U.S. officials began to stir unrest within the Liberal Party. Lloyd Axworthy, who had left politics but still retained influence among left-leaning Liberals, argued that the government was proceeding down a slippery slope. Axworthy said he found it extraordinary that McCallum was already talking about missile defence as a done deal, "and now we're setting up teams to do the planning on it without any public debate, without Parliamentary approval, without engaging the public," he told the *Toronto Star*.

From January 2003 onward, missile defence seemed to have tremendous political momentum, and each time a member of the government discussed the topic, the public was left with the impression that Canada's joining missile defence was "a done deal," and all that remained was working out the final details, followed by a formal announcement.

But in February 2003, a different political decision was looming large before the government: whether or not to join the U.S.-led invasion of Iraq. Missile defence was nearly eclipsed by the debates on the validity of the war, whether or not there would be a UN resolution endorsing the invasion, and under what conditions Canada would contribute military forces.

On February 15, several hundred thousand Canadians from all walks of life attended demonstrations against the anticipated invasion. More than a hundred thousand marched in Montreal alone— one of the largest demonstrations in Canadian history. The Canadian protests were part of a global day of protest that drew millions of people into the streets of major cities and national capitals around the world, especially in Europe. The BBC estimated that between six and ten million people joined anti-war demonstrations in eight hundred cities in sixty countries.

By March it was clear that the UN Security Council was not going to endorse the U.S. invasion of Iraq. On March 17, Prime Minister

Chrétien stood in the House of Commons and announced that, without a UN resolution, Canada would not join the invasion of Iraq.

It was a popular decision and it won a standing ovation from his caucus. Polls showed strong support for the anti-war decision, and public support actually increased as time passed and the U.S. invaded Iraq with only a handful of allied countries.

But business groups complained loudly that the decision not to join the United States would harm relations between the two countries. To many ordinary people this was a shameless demonstration of how business leaders were prepared to put concerns about their bottom line above the interests of global peace and stability, not to mention the lives of Canadian soldiers, who would have been stuck in the Iraq "quagmire."

In April the Canadian aerospace industry pressed the government hard to join the shield soon, so that they could win lucrative contracts to help build the system—before it was too late. In a letter to Prime Minister Chrétien, as reported in the *Globe and Mail*, an official from the Canadian Aerospace Industries Association wrote, "I urge you to convey to the American administration, at the earliest opportunity possible, that Canada will join with our strongest ally in this endeavour to strengthen the national security of our two nations." The organization comprises the largest high-tech corporations in Canada, including Bombardier and Derek H. Burney's company, CAE Inc.

Ron Kane, the vice-president of policy and research for the lobby group, told the *Globe* that "if we don't commit over the next couple of months, we'll be shut out." Kane admitted that his eagerness to join the system quickly was prompted by a meeting he had had with U.S. ambassador Paul Cellucci: "His message was that there was a very short window."

Canada's joining the U.S. missile-defence system was seen by many business leaders as a way to "kiss and make up" with George W. Bush. Proponents argued that the Americans were going ahead with the system anyway, since they didn't need Canadian territory or funding.

* * *

On the morning of April 29, 2003, I went to my doorstep to pick up my *Globe and Mail*, and was presented with a prominent opinion column under the headline, "Say No to Missile Defence." It was the opening round in the coming battle.

The article was written by Lloyd Axworthy and Michael Byers, a Canadian professor at Duke University, who no doubt sensed that there were many people inside and outside government and the Liberal Party opposed to missile defence. These people needed the intellectual arguments to counter the "neo-conservative juggernaut" from the Bush administration, "the push from Paul Cellucci, the U.S. ambassador-turned-proconsul," and the "Chicken Littles" of the business community who feared economic retaliation from the United States.

"Chalk up yet another political casualty of the Iraq war: Canada's impending loss of an independent voice in matters of peace and security," the article began. "Participating in missile defence would culminate in an effort by our armed forces to achieve complete 'interoperability.' The benefits to our generals are obvious: increased expenditures and the opportunity to work with the world's most powerful military force."

Axworthy and Byers pointed out that the reliability of the system was just as "unproven" as the missile threat to Canada. Joining the system would also run counter to Canada's long-held advocacy for arms control, and "condone the Bush administration's preference for military and technological, rather than co-operative, solutions to threats posed by weapons of mass destruction." Even more, it would "discredit any future efforts by our negotiators to secure a treaty setting limits on military space developments."

But perhaps more powerful for the Liberal caucus than any pressure from Washington to join missile defence was Paul Martin's endorsement of the system. With Martin clearly the favoured candidate to replace Jean Chrétien, every Liberal MP who wanted to remain in Cabinet, or ever dreamed of being appointed a Cabinet minister, jumped behind Martin's position on missile defence.

The head that snapped the quickest to attention was the former missile defence skeptic Foreign Affairs Minister Bill Graham.

Practically overnight Graham became a missile defence convert; he and Defence Minister John McCallum were the team to sell missile defence to their Cabinet—and caucus—colleagues.

McCallum and Graham sensed early in the public debate that the weaponization of space, and the missile-defence system's likelihood of employing space weapons in the future, was the greatest obstacle to winning the support of their caucus colleagues and the public.

To further the government's support of missile defence, government political leaders began to try to separate the space-weapons issue from missile defence, essentially arguing that Canada could join missile defence, and then exert influence on the United States to prevent them from weaponizing space. "We've clearly been against weaponization in space and any discussions we would have with the United States about any form of defence of North America would include that principled position," Bill Graham told reporters in early May 2003.

But later that week the spokesperson for the Pentagon's Missile Defense Agency contradicted Graham, saying the U.S. missile shield would be using space-based weapons in the future. Rick Lehner said in an interview that plans for space-based interceptors—orbiting missiles that could collide with enemy missiles shortly after launch—were in the concept-design phase, but testing could begin in 2008. "These would be small, non-explosive interceptors that would collide with a target," Lehner said.

Discussions in Cabinet continued through the spring, to May 2003. Graham and McCallum argued that, without Canada's decision to join missile defence, control over the system could not be placed under the joint Canada–U.S. NORAD command. "If missile defence becomes an exclusively American project and thus remains outside of NORAD, the role and relevance of this important partnership, so crucial for our participation in the defence of North America, will come into question," Bill Graham said.

A majority of Cabinet were reportedly in favour of the talks, but heritage minister and party leadership candidate Sheila Copps, as well as at least one other Cabinet member, were squarely opposed.

A number of backbench MPs began to raise their concerns as well. A letter by John Godfrey that circulated throughout the caucus raised pointed questions, including: "Does the current and projected missile threat to Canada justify involvement in the U.S. deployment of NMD [National Missile Defence]? Would Canada consider the placement of interceptor missiles or NMD-specific radar on its territory? If the U.S. government does weaponize space, would our government withdraw from NMD? How?"

But missile-defence proponents could claim public support for their position. A poll taken by SES Research in mid-May found that a majority of Canadians supported the U.S. missile shield plan. SES Research asked a thousand Canadians whether they supported Canada participating in a space-based missile shield. Sixty-one percent said they either strongly or somewhat supported Canada playing a role, while 24 percent were either somewhat or strongly opposed to it.

On May 29, the debate on whether to start negotiations ended. Defence Minister John McCallum stood in the House of Commons and announced, "Today, Mr. Speaker, I am pleased to announce that the government has decided to enter into discussions with the United States on Canada's participation in ballistic missile defence."

McCallum put forward a number of objectives for the government in the negotiations. The first was the protection of Canadian lives, and he argued that joining could ensure the system would defend Canada: "It is the responsibility of the government to do its due diligence to ensure that the system is set up and that the system will operate in such a way as to afford Canadians equal protection from such a threat as the protection that is afforded to Americans."

The second was to ensure that the operation of the missile-defence system was placed inside NORAD: "Up until now, up until today Canada has not expressed an interest in participating in ballistic missile defence and therefore the Americans were going along without us, not in NORAD because NORAD is binational, but rather in [the U.S.-only] Northern Command. . . . We will be suggesting that ballistic missile defence be lodged in NORAD."

The third objective was to exert influence over the decision by the

Americans to weaponize space: "Mr. Speaker, there is uncertainty in the United States as to whether the United States will or will not at some point proceed with the weaponization of space ... If we are part of ballistic missile defence, then at least we will be inside the tent and be able to make our views known in an attempt to influence the outcome of this U.S. decision."

Over time these objectives were to shift to include winning contracts for Canadian industry. In February 2004, James Wright, a senior foreign affairs official, would tell the Commons Foreign Affairs Committee that the government's objectives were to defend Canadians, ensure a key role for NORAD, and win industrial opportunities for Canada. "It is in Canada's national and strategic interest to be involved in any decisions concerning the defence of North America," he said. It was notable that any talk of preventing space weapons had disappeared.

Defence Minister McCallum had high expectations of the smooth conduct of negotiations in the summer of 2003. He expected that negotiations could be completed "in about a hundred days" and a decision could be made on whether or not to participate in the fall.

This was to be the first of many deadlines that the government would miss, as a final decision would be delayed repeatedly until well into 2005, a full twenty-one months after negotiations began in June 2003.

The day after McCallum announced the commencement of talks between Canada and the United States, while attending a G8 meeting in St Petersburg, Russia, Prime Minister Chrétien said, "We are talking at this point about the defence from missiles. It is not the weaponization of space. It is establishing a defence system to protect North America." He told reporters, "There will not be a program in which we will participate if it is to be the weaponization of space." This was remarkably inconsistent with what his foreign-affairs officials were saying.

In Washington, D.C., State Department spokesperson Charles Barclay reacted positively to the decision: "We think it is positive. We've had our differences with Canada over Iraq, sometimes there are differences in opinion on macroeconomic issues, but we have a long-standing security relationship with Canada which will be furthered by Canada's decision to begin discussions about a Canadian role in missile defence. It's a welcome move."

The U.S. general in charge of NORAD also had high praise for the Canadian decision to begin talks. "The sooner Canadians get on board, the more likely [Canadian] aerospace industries will be able to reap the benefits," General Ralph Eberhard told a meeting of the Winnipeg Chamber of Commerce.

Despite the praise from the Unites States, Jean Chrétien might well have felt relieved that he did not have to make the decision on missile defence, since his retirement was imminent. His decision to not join the invasion of Iraq would be the last item entered on the historical record during his tenure in the prime minister's chair.

At least one political commentator, acknowledging the bad blood between Chrétien and Paul Martin, commented that the missile-defence decision was a political hand grenade that Chrétien handed Martin on his way out the door.

Discomfort in the Liberal caucus about the government's decision to start negotiations broke into the open on June 4 during an important vote in parliament. Canadian Alliance leader Stephen Harper, who would become prime minister in 2006, introduced a motion to "support giving NORAD responsibility for the command of any system developed to defend North America against ballistic missiles." The NDP and the Bloc Québécois, both opponents of missile defence, voted against the motion, but it still passed with a majority from the Canadian Alliance and the Liberals. However, thirty-eight Liberal MPs voted against the motion, in defiance of the party's position on the issue. The division would plague the party for almost two years, through the entire debate on the issue.

Paul Martin's performance on this first test of his mettle on missile defence was very revealing. When the votes were being cast on the Canadian Alliance's pro-missile-defence motion, Paul Martin was not at his seat in the House of Commons.

Where was Paul Martin? Reporters found him wandering the halls just outside the Commons chamber, obviously hoping to avoid having to cast his vote. It was the first of many dodges Paul Martin would make on missile defence.

Stephen Harper seized on Martin's indecision. "As is typically the case, Paul had to keep a foot in both camps and not take a position," said Harper. "I know this guy has a huge lead in the polls, but Canadians are going to have to ask themselves if they really want a prime minister who can never make a decision on anything."

* * *

The moves in parliament prompted our organization to take action. "Within days a federal Cabinet decision could trap Canada into permanently supporting the U.S. military's missile defence scheme," Maude Barlow of the Council of Canadians wrote in a letter we sent to thousands of people on our e-mail contact list. "And Canadians won't know what hit them because Defence Minister John McCallum is keeping negotiations under wraps."

We sent this letter from Maude to our contact list just after Remembrance Day in November 2003. When McCallum had announced the start of talks at the end of May 2003, he predicted that a decision could be made by Cabinet "in a hundred days." By the time September rolled around there was still no decision, despite several meetings between Canadian and American officials.

"I'm hoping that sometime in the fall we might be able to come back to Cabinet, but we are talking about very important issues and I'm not going to rush it," McCallum told reporters. "There's the issue of whether or not Americans will want any Canadian territory—it seems unlikely at the moment, it may be the case at some future date ... There's the issue of what possible contribution in kind or in money Canada might be asked to make; there's the critical issue for Canada of ensuring the protection afforded to Canadians is no less than the protection afforded to Americans." A U.S. official reportedly confirmed that "territorial coverage" of the missile shield was at the centre of negotiations between the United States and Canada.

But the unstated issue was space weapons. The government had staked their support of missile defence on the fact that the initial system being deployed did not include space-based weapons, such as orbiting interceptor missiles. All of the interceptors would be on the ground in Alaska and California, or put aboard warships.

The U.S. government was less than helpful as the Canadian government attempted to create this distinction. Statements, reports, and funding for space weapons in the United States continued to undermine Liberal assurances that there would be no weapons in space, and aided NDP and Bloc Québécois claims to the contrary. In fact, the NDP's labelling of the system as "Bush's Star Wars" stuck in people's minds, much to the frustration of missile-defence proponents.

McCallum's argument that being inside the tent would help influence U.S. decision-making on space weapons proved to be without foundation. In fact, concerns about space weapons prompted some U.S. officials to keep Canadians out of the system to avoid having to contend with our discomfort with space weapons. In April 2003, James Roche, secretary of the U.S. Air Force, had told American military officers at a space conference that U.S. allies would have "no veto" over key programs needed to defend America. If the U.S. administration concluded it needed space weapons to defend the country, then complaints from Canada would fall on deaf ears.

November arrived, Paul Martin won the Liberal leadership race, and still there was no decision on missile defence. If some framework agreement had been reached behind closed doors, Jean Chrétien was going to leave the final decision to Paul Martin. Just like all of those people attending that conference of power-brokers at the Château Laurier, we were all waiting to see what Paul Martin's first move as prime minister would be.

I felt that, if Paul Martin was going to vote "yes" on joining missile defence, December 2003 or January 2004 was the time for him to do it. His political capital was worth a fortune, as polls showed, he had a huge lead over all the other parties. Public opinion on missile defence was not fully formed as yet, so he could afford to take a small hit on his popularity with some people by making the decision to join.

It would not have been a surprise to anyone if Martin had joined the missile-shield plan. He very clearly campaigned for the Liberal leadership on a platform of improving Canada–U.S. relations, and he made no bones about the fact that he thought Canada's joining missile defence would help that effort.

While there was some dissension in his caucus, many of those voices could be silenced or managed. Some of them were quieted with the promise of Cabinet postings. Such was the case with John Godfrey. Godfrey had been outspoken on the issue and had even written an opinion piece for the *Globe and Mail* in the summer of 2003 that was critical of missile defence. But Martin brought him into Cabinet and made him responsible for municipalities as Minister of State for Infrastructure and Communities. The result? No more op-eds or any public comments on missile defence from Mr. Godfrey.

If critics couldn't be co-opted, they could be driven out. Such was the fate of heritage minister and party-leadership rival Sheila Copps, who was dropped from Cabinet and then lost the nomination for her Hamilton riding in a very bitter and controversial nomination race. She still maintains it was won unfairly by the Martin-backed candidate, Tony Valeri.

As for the rest of the Liberal backbenchers, the prospect of an election in the near future would have been enough to force a consensus in support of their pro-missile-defence party leader. For Martin, joining missile defence might have seemed like tearing off a Band-Aid—a brief moment of pain, but over quickly. Certainly a quick decision is what Tom d'Aquino was pressing for at the Château Laurier. Joining missile defence early in his first term as prime minister would have won Paul Martin accolades in Washington and in Canada's corporate board-rooms.

That's why, during the transition from Chrétien to Martin, we all awaited the dreaded decision. In November, Lloyd Axworthy wrote in the *Globe and Mail*, "A decision on Canada's role [in ballistic-missile defence] will be made within the next couple of weeks, after Mr. Martin becomes Liberal leader, but before he becomes formally accountable for Canadian foreign policy. This is the first test of his stewardship."

In December, Paul Martin announced his choices for his first Cabinet, and our worst fears were confirmed. David Pratt, an MP from a riding just outside downtown Ottawa, was chosen by Martin as defence minister. Columnist John Ibbitson wrote of David Pratt: "Mr. Pratt opposed the Chrétien government's refusal to join the coalition [to invade Iraq]. He is a firm believer in the need for Canada to sign on to the continental missile defence system. He strongly supports a larger and better-equipped military. He is as Americanophillic as you can get."

The writing was on the wall.

* * *

I had first met David Pratt back in March 2003, when he was chair of the Commons Standing Committee on Defence and Veterans Affairs. I was invited to make a presentation before the all-party committee on Canada's defence policy.

Parliament has many committees, each generally corresponding to a government department. Unlike their American counterparts, these committees are mostly advisory in nature—but they do have influence. They can invite witnesses—including department officials and the minister himself or herself—to make presentations, and can publish reports. These reports frequently garner media attention, which influences government policy.

I had drawn some attention to the Polaris Institute in December 2002 with the publication of my first report on defence policy, *Breaking Rank: A Citizens' Review of Canada's Military Spending*. The report's central finding contradicted the defence lobby's think-tanks by arguing that Canada's military spending was already high by global standards and that pressure from the United States and special-interest groups was driving it further upward.

The defence committee meets in the East Block building on Parliament Hill. When I arrived at the meeting room, I was greeted by a homemade sign taped to the door that read "The War Room." I expected to walk in and see Peter Sellers and George C. Scott sitting around a black table looking at big maps on the wall, as in Stanley Kubrick's anti-war film *Dr. Strangelove*. No one can forget Peter Sellers's line when he breaks up an altercation between two generals:

"Gentlemen! You can't fight in here—this is the war room!"

It was a gruelling few hours. I was the only witness testifying before the committee. The way the meetings work is that members from each party take turns asking questions of the witness. I got nothing but sneering remarks and aggressive questioning from the Liberals, the Conservatives, and the Canadian Alliance members.

At least the NDP and the Bloc Québécois had a few questions. Not surprisingly, I shared many views with Bill Blaikie of the NDP, as I did with the Bloc Québécois's defence critic Claude Bachand from the riding of Saint-Jean. Bachand in particular was, and remains, a very effective member of that defence committee. In the House itself, he posed many of the Bloc's questions on missile defence to the prime minister.

David Pratt was another matter. It was during his tenure as chair of the Commons defence committee that he came to be seen as a hawk in the Liberal Party. Under his leadership the committee published the report *Facing Our Responsibilities: The States of Readiness of the Canadian Forces*, which called for a whopping 50 percent increase to military spending in three years, moving toward a doubling of spending beyond that—an amount higher than has ever been allocated to military spending in Canadian history. Pratt, as mentioned, also disagreed with Jean Chrétien's decision to not join the U.S. invasion of Iraq. When the prime minister made that announcement in the House of Commons, members of the Liberal caucus had all jumped to their feet with applause—except David Pratt.

No doubt David Pratt was viewed by the defence lobby as their Golden Boy. The lobby had no love for then–defence minister, John McCallum, and Pratt was being groomed by the government for the role.

In June 2003, I attended the annual CANSEC arms show at the Congress Centre in Ottawa. Dozens of companies were exhibiting their military technology, such as automated machine guns, missiles, spy drones—an entire armoury. The aisles were filled with military and other government personnel, who were collecting leaflets and listening to the arms dealers' sales pitches.

At the luncheon, I saw David Pratt seated at the General Dynamics corporate table. General Dynamics is the sixth-largest armsmaker in the world, and likely the largest in Canada as well, after their recent purchase of General Motors's tank-manufacturing plant in London, Ontario. At General Dynamics's table, Pratt was surrounded by the other military brass, and of course the corporation's executives.

This was the man to whom Paul Martin handed both the keys to Canada's military and the missile-defence file. It spoke volumes about the direction in which Paul Martin intended to take the military: straight into the arms of the Pentagon. David Pratt was the man to do the job.

* * *

It remains one of the great mysteries of the missile-defence issue: In light of all this, why didn't Paul Martin join the U.S. missile-defence system in January 2004?

Everything was in his favour—supportive polls, a united caucus, pro-missile-defence ministers of defence and foreign affairs, support from the bureaucracy, big-business backing, a mandate from the Liberal Party on the issue, months of negotiations completed, and no election call expected until the spring …

Even more important, Martin was about to hold his first face-to-face meeting with George W. Bush at a trade meeting in Monterrey, Mexico. If Martin had truly wanted to "rebuild" relations with the United States, what could be better than delivering a "yes" decision on missile defence to the president at their first meeting?

Fresh from his first Cabinet meeting in January, David Pratt came out swinging. He charged that opponents of missile defence, especially NDP leader, Jack Layton, were stirring up false fears in the public. "When Jack Layton talks about Star Wars, what he's doing is parading his lack of knowledge to the Canadian people of the system. He's trying to scaremonger and frighten Canadians," he told the *Ottawa Citizen*.

Pratt argued that the system would not put weapons in space. "It's really a fairly modest system that is being contemplated, particularly if you go back to the Reagan Star Wars initiative." He added that the space weapons issue is "so far off into the future that it's not a concern for us at this point—it's not going to be an issue that has to be dealt with by this government or the next government or probably even the government after that."

Now with David Pratt taking charge of the negotiations, a key objective of the government's negotiating demands had been quietly dropped. Back in May 2003, Bill Graham had stated that the government would not compromise its stand against the weaponization of space, and McCallum had told the House of Commons that one of his main objectives was to convince the Americans not to deploy them.

But David Pratt omitted the demand for assurances from the Americans that they would not use space weapons for the system. "Instead," reported the *Globe and Mail*, "Canada and the United States have decided to hold talks on current plans to create a land-and sea-based system, while agreeing that any decision on weapons in space is more than a decade away." The *Globe* reported that Pratt intended to send a letter to his U.S. counterpart, Secretary of Defense Donald Rumsfeld, to add greater formality to the ongoing talks.

The day after Pratt accused critics of scaremongering, the headline on the front page of the *Ottawa Citizen* revealed what Pratt, Graham, McCallum, Martin, and Chrétien had known all along, "Missile Shield Risks Militarizing Space: DND." *Citizen* reporter David Pugliese had obtained a Canadian military report through an Access to Information request that revealed that the Department of National Defence had warned senior government leaders that the system would lead to space weapons.

The report had been produced in the spring of 2003, before the government decided to proceed with official negotiations but during the time that ministers Graham and McCallum, and even Prime Minister Chrétien, were denying that missile defence would weaponize space. The study concluded that "A significant risk associated with BMD from the non-proliferation and disarmament perspective is its reinforcement of trends toward the weaponization of outer space."

Pugliese had called me about the report while he was writing his story. He included my reaction in his article: "Steve Staples, a defence analyst with the Ottawa-based Polaris Institute, said Prime Minister Paul Martin's desire to have Canada join the missile shield has little to do with protecting the country, but is designed to smooth over strained relations with the U.S., and the Bush administration in particular. 'What's happening here is that missile defence is being designed to protect us from rogue U.S. trade policies, not rogue nations,' Mr. Staples said."

David Pugliese's investigative reporting provided vital information to the Canadian public. Most defence reporters exhibited so little curiosity that they appeared to be not much more than scribes for the military establishment. But the information provided by Pugliese, and a handful of others, kept chipping away at the government's arguments.

Liberal backbenchers were furious to learn of the DND report on space weapons, and of Pratt's intention to write a letter to U.S. Secretary of Defense Donald Rumsfeld. Liberal MP Bonnie Brown questioned whether Washington could be trusted to provide accurate information: "When they tell you something, will it be true? There is the whole question of what they told us about Iraq, which has proven to be untrue."

Brown and fellow Liberal MPs Marlene Jennings and Charles Caccia said the government should drop its plan to exchange letters with the United States, arguing that Defence Minister Pratt failed to consult widely with caucus members. "I don't know any numbers of MPs opposed, but I think that this minister is sticking his neck out pretty far without checking with us," said Ms. Brown. "He has been chair of the defence committee and as such has developed, in his few years in public life, a very military-influenced view of the world."

* * *

On January 13, 2004, Paul Martin got on a plane and went to Monterrey, Mexico, for the Summit of the Americas, where he would meet with other hemispheric leaders and the president of the United States. I got on a plane myself, and with media accreditation in hand, also went to Monterrey (I was reporting for the online newspaper *rabble.ca*).

Government officials had been telling reporters that missile defence would be touched upon during the meeting. My goal in Monterrey was to monitor the prime minister's statements closely, especially anything related to missile defence.

Citizens' groups frequently use media accreditation and press passes to gain access to the proceedings of government meetings. It is a common practice, mostly because our organizations, along with the public in general, are completely excluded from the process—unlike business groups, which regularly receive special access. I travelled with a colleague from the Council of Canadians, Guy Caron, who was covering the group's work on Canada–U.S. relations.

I was amazed at how much control journalists allowed the prime minister's office to hold over them. They were carted around the city like cattle on government-supplied buses, wrote their stories on government-supplied computers in a government-supplied media room, and followed the government-supplied daily agenda to the minute. The prime minister's office even kindly included breaks for the reporters in the daily schedule.

Of course, the reporters trade their physical freedom for access. As Guy and I quickly learned, if you are not part of the official press pool, you are out of the loop. But we did find out when and where the prime minister was meeting Bush, so we hired a taxi and managed to get to the Presidente Inter-Continental Hotel where Bush was staying in time for the meeting.

Once we cleared the phalanx of security guards and sniffer dogs at the door, Guy spotted Colin Powell walking through the lobby. Ambassador Paul Cellucci was there too. We found our fellow reporters waiting in a dark pub, where they had been corralled for the duration of Bush and Martin's meeting. Three reporters had been chosen by their peers to go and ask questions and record the leaders' answers. Of course, all the reporters knew each other from covering the prime minister and politics in Ottawa, so Guy and I stood out like sore thumbs.

"What are you guys doing here?" asked Susan Delacourt of the *Toronto Star*.

"We're journalists," I replied.

Later, Guy and I followed the few dozen journalists up to the press-conference room, where Paul Martin and Foreign Affairs Minister Bill Graham were to talk to the Canadian reporters directly following Martin's meeting with Bush. We didn't plan on disrupting the meeting; in fact, we wanted to hear what Martin had to say. Both Guy and I had been giving interviews to media back home in Canada, and I was scheduled to be on CBC Radio's national program *The Current* the next morning.

Graham entered the room first, then the prime minister. Martin stuck mainly to the trade issues, which at that time were cattle and softwood-lumber exports to the United States and juicy Iraqi reconstruction con-tracts for Canadian companies. The reporters asked questions in response to the briefing, but missile defence was never mentioned. The press conference ended and everyone left.

When asked about it later, Prime Minister Martin said the missile-defence issue didn't came up while he was meeting with Bush. The truth is that he knew support for missile defence was declining in Canadian public-opinion polls, and as one reporter pointed out, "The Americans know very well what issues are controversial in Canada and when to avoid talking about them publicly."

* * *

A few days after Martin's meeting with Bush, Defence Minister David Pratt sent a letter to Donald Rumsfeld. The letter stated that Canada was seeking the "closest possible participation" in missile defence, but it stopped short of actually expressing a desire to join.

This letter of January 15, 2004, said:

Dear Secretary Rumsfeld:

For decades the United States and Canada have been part-ners in the defence of North America, co-operating within the framework of the Ogdensburg Agreement, the North Atlantic Treaty, and the North American Aerospace Defense Command (NORAD) to preserve our mutual security. In light of the grow-ing threat involving the proliferation of ballistic missiles and weapons of mass destruction, we should explore extending this partnership to include co-operation in missile defence, as an appropriate response to these new threats and as a useful complement to our non-proliferation efforts.

A key focus of our co-operation in missile defence should be through NORAD, which has served us well since 1958. NORAD's long-standing global threat warning and attack assessment role can make an important contribution to the execution of the missile defence mission. We believe that our two nations should move on an expedited basis to amend the NORAD agreement to take into account NORAD's contribution to the missile defence mission.

It is our intent to negotiate in the coming months a Missile Defence Framework Memorandum of Understanding (MOU) with the United States with the objective of including Canada as a participant in the current U.S. missile defence program and expanding and enhancing information exchange. We believe this should provide a mutually beneficial framework to ensure the closest possible involvement and insight for Canada, both government and industry, in the U.S. missile defence program. Such an MOU could also help pave the way for increased government-to-government and industry-to-industry co-operation on missile defence that we should seek to foster between our countries.

We understand the United States is prepared to consult with Canada on operational planning issues associated with the defence of North America. I propose that our staffs work together over the coming months to identify opportunities and mechanisms for such consultations and Canada's contributions.

The technical extent of protection afforded by the U.S. ballistic missile defence system will evolve over time, and our bilateral co-operation in this area should also evolve. We should continue to explore appropriate technical, political and financial arrangements related to the potential defence of Canada and the United States against missile attack, within the framework of our laws. Our staffs should discuss ways in which Canada could contribute to this effort.

If this overall framework for co-operation that I have proposed meets with your approval, I would appreciate hearing back from you at your earliest convenience.

Yours sincerely, The Honourable David Pratt, P.C., M.P.

To which Donald Rumsfeld replied:

Dear Minister Pratt:

Thank you for your recent letter regarding cooperation between the United States and Canada on missile defense.

As you noted in your letter, the United States and Canada have been partners in the defense of North America for over 50 years. In light of the threat involving the proliferation of ballistic missiles, I agree that we should seek to expand our cooperation in the area of missile defense.

I am supportive of the approach to missile defense cooperation that you outlined in your letter and agree that this should be the basis on which we move forward.

Thank you again for your letter. I look forward to continuing the long-standing defense cooperation between the United States and Canada.

Sincerely, Donald Rumsfeld, U.S. Secretary of Defense

According to several former diplomats I spoke to about Pratt's letter, it was unusual that a letter concerning negotiations on this issue would come from the defence minister, and not the foreign affairs minister. In the government hierarchy, the foreign affairs department is the lead agency for international negotiations and the defence department plays second fiddle. But in this case it was clearly the military leading the charge.

In addition to that, the letter was so poorly constructed and argued that experts assumed that David Pratt had actually written it himself, rather than using a text provided by skilled and experienced negotiators, as is typically done. For instance, Pratt's admission that his goal was to join the system effectively removed any bargaining power he might have had in negotiations with the Americans. No one tells a car dealer, "My goal is to leave here with this car, so let's start talking about the price I'm going to pay."

All of this raised the question: Were the Americans pressuring Canada to join, or was Canada pleading to be let in?

My sense was that something was going wrong with the negotiations that McCallum and Graham had initiated in June, and which had been going on for eight months. In the press release that accompanied the release of the letter, Pratt said, "This step will help to move forward discussions on possible Canadian participation in the missile defence of North America. It sets out a clear path for future negotiations, and will allow Canada to have access to the information about missile defence that we will need to make a decision on participation."

Why did David Pratt say that the letter "will allow Canada to have access to the information about missile defence that we will need to make a decision on participation"? Were the American negotiators not providing the information the Canadians needed or wanted? Did Pratt have to appeal to their boss, Rumsfeld, to move the negotiations forward?

In an interview, Pratt admitted that Canadian negotiators were being denied important information. "There have been very constructive discussions, no doubt about that." He told the *Ottawa Citizen.* "There's a lot of fairly sensitive technical information that we want to have access to before making a final decision on this, [such as] ... which cities are going to be covered and which are not [and] the trajectory of various possible missiles" through Canadian airspace.

Pratt said he hoped he could send a recommendation to Cabinet before October. This would be more than a year after his predecessor had expected to achieve the same objective when negotiations started in June 2003.

"Maybe the delay was something else. Could it be a stalling tactic?" I thought at the time. The Liberals are well known for polling the public repeatedly, and fashioning every policy and announcement around polling information. Were there private polls warning them about missile defence?

* * *

There's a saying, "The higher the pedestal, the farther the fall." I doubt that Paul Martin was thinking about that as he watched the Liberal majority government he'd been handed crumble to a minority government in June 2004.

During the election, he had presented himself as a champion of Canadian sovereignty and global peacekeeping, largely in order to cast Stephen Harper in the role of a knuckle-dragging, Bush-loving warmonger.

Our campaign against Canada joining missile defence was already under way before the election, and we were working hard to make it an issue during the campaign. The issue was picked up by the parties. When confronted with his support for Bush's Star Wars scheme by Jack Layton of the NDP, Martin professed his opposition to weapons in space and his plan to hire five thousand more peacekeeping troops.

It was ironic that the man who had campaigned for the Liberal leadership on a plan to improve relations with the Bush administration had successfully portrayed himself as "Captain Canada" during the election, stirring up all kinds of nationalist, peace-loving sentiments.

The Liberals lost many MPs in the election, but the biggest surprise for us was the defeat of David Pratt in Nepean–Carleton. Pratt's loss was particularly humiliating, because he was beaten by a twenty-five-year-old political neophyte, Pierre Poilievre of the Conservatives. It seemed surprising that the Conservatives won in a riding held by a conservative Liberal Cabinet member.

But a closer examination shows that it was really the NDP that had defeated Pratt. The NDP performed better in this riding than expected, drawing enough votes from the Liberals to allow the Conservatives to win a majority of votes. Pratt lost by 3,790 votes. The NDP candidate, Phil Brown, garnered 6,097 votes from his campaign, which focused almost exclusively on Pratt's support for missile defence. Outside his last Cabinet meeting a few days after the election, David Pratt spoke to reporters and tried to put on a brave face, admitting that he did not expect "a hook from the Left."

3

THE CANADIAN CAMPAIGN TO OPPOSE MISSILE DEFENCE

It must have been the worst press conference I had ever organized. "How many journalists attended?" my colleague Jillian Skeet asked me over my cell phone from her home office in Vancouver. Jillian is a well-known writer and longtime peace activist who was working on the campaign against missile defence with me.

"Only one," I replied.

"From the *Toronto Star*, the *Globe and Mail*?" asked Jillian hopefully.

"No, she was more of a student journalist," I replied.

"Oh ... from a student newspaper ... *The Varsity* at the University of Toronto?" Jillian suggested.

"Well, sort of . . . actually no, she's from a student *on-line* newspaper ... " I told her. There was an awkward silence on the line.

It was March 18, 2004, and the grand launch of our newly formed Canadian Campaign to Oppose Missile Defence had received far, far less fanfare that we had hoped. That morning I had flown from Ottawa to Toronto for a press conference to release an open letter to Paul Martin, urging him not to commit Canada to joining the U.S. missile defence system. It had been signed by a long list of famous Canadians.

The letter had been written by a small group of people involved in the campaign, including Jillian. It was very eloquent, and captured the essence of our campaign's opposition to missile defence.

An Open Letter to Prime Minister Martin

We, the undersigned, are deeply alarmed that our government continues to pursue Canadian involvement in the development of the U.S. missile-defence system.

Canadian involvement in U.S. missile defence would undermine decades of Canadian efforts to rid the world of nuclear weapons. It would represent our acquiescence and willingness to become an active participant in a permanent nuclear future. As such, it would directly collide with the wishes of the Canadian people, who have expressed overwhelming support for nuclear disarmament.

It would require the reversal of a 30-year Canadian policy opposing the weaponization of space. The Bush administration's plans for missile defence expressly include the placement of space-based weaponry. The most recent U.S. budget specifies an intent to develop a space-based missile "test bed," beginning as early as 2005.

While we understand the government's desire to improve Canada–U.S. relations, we firmly believe that the political and economic benefits of Canadian integration in missile defence would be far outweighed by the long-term negative consequences for global security, and for Canadian sovereignty over future foreign affairs and defence matters.

The pursuit of missile defence is enormously expensive, with current expenditures in the range of US$8–12 billion per year and climbing. It is based on unproven technology and has dangerous implications for strategic stability. A new global arms race is a likely consequence, as existing nuclear powers seek to maintain a credible deterrence by strengthening their retaliatory arsenals of missiles and warheads.

By devoting vast resources to developing a missile shield, the United States is ignoring the real causes of insecurity, and is likely to aggravate existing grievances. Security for us all would be much better served by rejuvenating multilateral efforts to stop the spread of nuclear weapons and uphold international law, and by addressing the root causes of conflict and terrorism, such as civil strife, global inequality, and environmental degradation.

As a good neighbour, Canada should be working to convince the U.S. that true and lasting security cannot be achieved through military might. No missile shield could ever ensure the safety of North America. If the front door is closed, someone will find a way in through the back.

True security can only be achieved by establishing relationships of mutual respect and co-operation, free of exploitation, with nations and peoples throughout the world.

That is what we, as Canadians, have always believed and proudly stood for. And that is the kind of Canada that we want now and in the future.

Mr. Martin, we implore you—and all Canadians—to keep Canada out of missile defence.

Jillian had spent the last three weeks doing a wonderful job of gathering the list of Canadian celebrities to sign the letter. Through telephone calls, e-mails, and in some cases special-delivery letters to places scattered around the globe, Jillian had invited 207 well-known Canadians to join our cause. Only a handful declined to add their names, mostly because they felt they did not know enough about the issue to legitimately sign the letter.

Our press-release headline trumpeted, "Canada's Stars Urge Paul Martin to 'Keep Canada Out of Star Wars.'" Among our stellar roll of signatories were winners of the Nobel Prize, of Grammy Awards, and of the Order of Canada. They included: Bryan Adams, Pierre Berton, Sarah McLachlan, Michael Ondaatje, Shirley Douglas, David Suzuki, Stompin' Tom Connors, John Polanyi, Susan Aglukark, and Raffi, among others.

After its release, it was posted on the Internet, and more than fifteen thousand Canadians signed the letter as well. Each time someone signed his or her name, a copy was e-mailed to the prime minister's office.

When I arrived at the downtown Toronto hotel where we had announced we would hold our press conference to launch the letter, I was greeted by a group of signatories who had agreed to speak: the brilliant pianist Anton Kuerti; Ernie Regehr; the former moderator of the United Church of Canada, Senator Lois Wilson; and the wonderful Canadian actress and social activist Shirley Douglas.

I watched the clock nervously, waiting for journalists to arrive. The clock ticked past the announced hour of the press conference: five minutes, ten minutes, finally twenty minutes passed as the five of us stood around in a roomful of empty chairs. If the hotel room hadn't been so high above the ground, I would have leapt out the window to end my embarrassment.

But when the sole student reporter arrived, it at least gave each of the speakers an opportunity to say what they had come to say. We gathered in a small circle, and one after another of our speakers made marvellously eloquent arguments for traditional Canadian values and the need for our country to chart its own course in the world.

Later I learned that our dismal turn-out was largely because we had chosen a poorly located hotel to hold the press conference. As well, local organizers were holding events in their cities and were drawing respectable media attention—especially in Halifax.

There was a small silver lining for me, because after our conference broke up, Shirley Douglas invited me to have lunch with her before I went back to the airport for the return flight to Ottawa. She took me to a little bistro on Queen Street, just down the street from the hotel.

She wanted to talk about the campaign and the missile-defence issue, but it was all I could do to resist asking her about her fascinating career and her famous family. She is the daughter of Tommy Douglas, who was the founder of what is today the NDP, was widely acknowledged as the "father of Medicare," and was recently voted the "Greatest Canadian" by tens of thousands of CBC-TV viewers. Shirley took a different path from her father and became a Hollywood actress. Among her long list of film credits is the 1962 classic *Lolita* by director Stanley Kubrick, one of my favourite directors. She was for a time married to actor Donald Sutherland, and is the mother of the film and television actor Kiefer Sutherland.

Shirley is a committed activist, who is best known for her work defending public health care. But she is also a peace activist, another strong interest that she acquired from her father. While we were discussing the extent to which Canada's corporate elite and many politicians supported missile defence as a way to help the U.S. War on Terrorism, Shirley leaned closer to me and said, "You know, Steve, my father used to tell me, 'In the United States they have politicians who are hawks or doves, but in Canada we seem to have an awful lot of parrots.'"

As we were leaving the restaurant, we passed by a front table where comedian Rick Mercer was taking a break from filming his satirical CBC comedy program, *Monday Report*. "Hello, Rick," said Shirley, to which Rick replied "Hello ... Shirley," with a half-smile.

"We're signing a letter to the prime minister to urge him not to join George Bush's missile-defence plan, Rick. Maybe you'd like to join us," said Shirley, as she passed him a copy of our letter.

"That's great ... thanks ... " said Rick; he half-read it, and then tucked it in his pocket. I was somewhat surprised by his lukewarm response, since he is the CBC's best-known political satirist and iconoclast.

Shirley and I kept in touch over the duration of the campaign. Rick Mercer never did join his many colleagues in signing the letter, but he and I would to be in contact once more.

Almost a year later, the government would announce its decision to not join missile defence. The missile-defence lobby was furious, accusing Paul Martin of pandering to Quebec voters rather than "doing the right thing" and joining the U.S. missile shield.

One morning, about a week after the decision was announced and the CEOs were howling their outrage, I received calls from several people who were confused and alarmed by a sketch that Rick had performed on his show the night before. The callers felt he was supporting missile defence, or at least poking fun at its critics. So I sent a brief e-mail to the general mailbox of Rick's show, with the provocative subject line, "I can't believe the rumour going around about Rick." My message said, "I heard that Rick Mercer is actually in favour of missile defence. I can hardly believe it—is this true?" I received this reply from Rick himself later that night.

> Steven
>
> While I love the idea that there is a "rumour going around" about me, I can neither confirm nor deny it.
>
> I did a bit on the show implying that the Liberals said no to Missile Defense because of the programs polling numbers in Quebec; I suppose some people might have thought that meant I was gung-ho on Missile Defence. Of course some people may think Paul Martin's decision has nothing to do with the polls.
>
> Although it is my position that one would have no sense of humour to jump to the conclusion that I was pro missile defence, I can say this; I'm pretty damn sure it will never work.
>
> Rick Mercer

Our Toronto press conference, in addition to similar events in Halifax, Edmonton, and Vancouver, garnered coverage in about eighteen newspaper articles across the country. But we were disappointed that there was no television coverage, and in most cases the story was not considered a news story by editors. For instance, the *Calgary Herald* ran a brief article in the entertainment section of the newspaper with a photo of Stompin' Tom Connors, one of our signatories, below the headline "Tom Stomps on Bush Plan." Funny, but not exactly the coverage we had hoped for.

For months afterwards, Jillian, who had put so much work into gathering signatories, lamented that the missile-defence letter deserved much more attention than the media had given it. By September she had resolved to simply raise enough money to buy media space and have the letter and its list of well-known signatories placed in several daily newspapers. By appealing to the signatories themselves, many of whom were leaders of large organizations, Jillian quickly raised enough money to run the letter as a quarter-page ad in the *Toronto Star*, the *Ottawa Citizen*, and the Vancouver *Sun*.

Despite the less-than-resounding campaign media launch, the Canadian Campaign to Oppose Missile Defence was the start of an effective working relationship within a network of people who were committed to preventing Canada from joining George W. Bush's missile defence system.

Eventually we would develop a campaign strategy that operated in the streets and in the backrooms of parliament, on TV and over the Internet, until Paul Martin had no choice a year later but to throw in the towel and tell Bush that Canada would not be participating in the missile shield.

As my friend Michael Byers at Duke University told me when we first spoke in late 2003, "Steve, the more people know about missile defence, the more they will be opposed to it." He was right.

* * *

"I am getting calls from all over the country now," I said to Debbie Grisdale, executive director of the doctors' peace group Physicians for Global Survival. "Since the exchange of letters between Pratt and Rumsfeld, I've heard from peace coalitions in Halifax, Saskatoon, Winnipeg, Edmonton, Vancouver, and Victoria. What are you hearing?"

Debbie had been in touch with many of her own members, and agreed that the situation had shifted and there was a new sense of urgency amongst the peace movement. It was January 2004, and, although the two of us had been talking about a national movement to keep Canada out of missile defence for nearly a year, we had resigned ourselves to the fact that that it would have been like "pushing a rope" to get groups together—until now.

Debbie and I met with Senator Douglas Roche, who is a long-time member of the peace movement. From 1972 until 1984, prior to being appointed to the Senate in 1998, Doug Roche had been a Conservative member of parliament for Edmonton, and later was appointed Canada's ambassador for disarmament to the United Nations, where he chaired international negotiations at the UN Conference on Disarmament.

Doug has been a mentor to many young activists, and I count him as one of mine. Doug's moral conviction, informed by his experience as both a politician and a diplomat, provides him with a perspective on ways of achieving positive change that is unique among his peers.

"People are looking for leadership, or at least coordination, on missile defence," I reported to Doug and Debbie. "Generally, the message I'm hearing is that there is a sense of urgency because of the recent developments, mixed with optimism that the issue is being taken up by the NDP and many prominent people such as Lloyd Axworthy. Regional groups are looking for leadership and intelligence for a national strategy that they can plug in to—especially in light of the election."

It was clear that the country would be heading for a federal election in the coming months. With Paul Martin's arrival as prime minister on Jean Chrétien's retirement, all the parties were positioning themselves to head to the polls. "We need our own coalition of civil-society groups," Doug suggested. "And it is far better to have a coalition formed now, before the election, so that the media and Canadians see that there is an important group of Canadians opposed to BMD."

Doug was making two important points. One was that we needed to ensure that we created a non-partisan campaign; that is, the campaign could not be seen to be attached to any particular party. The other important point that Doug was making was that the campaign needed to begin well before the election, which was widely thought to be only a matter of months away.

Many organizations make the mistake of thinking that elections are a good time to introduce their issues. But there is very little political space during an election for extra-parliamentary groups to raise issues or contribute to the debate, let alone try to push their own issue to the top of the public agenda.

The truth is, as Prime Minister Kim Campbell once famously quipped, "an election is no time to discuss serious issues." Once an election is called, the media focuses almost exclusively on the party leaders, their statements on policy and comments about the other parties, and of course on public-opinion polls. After the televised debates, which are held in the last half of the campaign, it becomes a horse race. So, if we wanted missile defence to become a "top of mind" issue that would be covered in the election and commented upon by the party leaders, we needed to start early enough to create public interest in the issue so that the parties would have to respond by elaborating on their own positions and engaging in the debate. This would lead to media coverage.

"My suggestion is that the two of you, Debbie and Steve, produce a short paper on how you see such a coalition working. Then run it by the relevant groups. I will work with you in this effort," Doug added.

* * *

The idea of a coalition of citizen groups working on missile defence received a good response from the various civil-society groups across Canada in the days that followed.

On Thursday, February 5, 2004, we held our first conference call. On the line were people from across the country: Senator Doug Roche in Edmonton; Ernie Regehr in Waterloo; Peggy Mason in Ottawa; Michael Murphy in Saskatoon; Sheila Zurbrig and Colleen Ashford in Halifax; Stacy Chappel in Victoria; Martine Eloy in Montreal; Michael Byers in North Carolina; John Price, Elaine Hynes, and Irene MacInnis in Vancouver; finally me and Debbie, who was chairing the meeting. The meeting went very well, and I was very impressed with the range of skills and experience of the people who had come together: experts and activists, youth organizers and church leaders, veterans of Parliament Hill and street protests alike.

On that first call we approved a document that would set out our understanding of the political moment, our goals, and our objectives:

CANADIAN COALITION TO OPPOSE MISSILE DEFENCE (CCOMD)

The missile defence debate is at a critical juncture. The Canadian government has approved military-to-military talks with the Pentagon to achieve, in the words of Defence Minister

David Pratt, the closest possible participation in the U.S. missile shield.

But while the talks seem to be moving ever closer to such a conclusion, in the last few weeks the government has made several significant reversals, including delaying a decision until the fall—almost a year later than the original timetable, committing to a public and Parliamentary debate before a final decision is made instead of a decision by Cabinet alone, and most recently announcing that there is, in fact, no deadline for Canada to make its decision known to the United States despite saying previously that a decision was needed before October 1, 2004.

The United States Missile Defence Agency has taken two actions that put further pressure on the Canadian government.

First, the date for activating the missile defence shield has been advanced from September 30, 2004, to sometime in July 2004, a timetable that will interfere with a potential election expected in the spring.

Second, the Bush administration's FY 2005/06 budget request submitted to Congress on February 2, 2004, included $47 million for technological development of "advanced, lightweight, space-based (missile) interceptor components," according to the U.S. Missile Defence Agency. The inclusion of space-based weapons would violate Canada's long-standing opposition to the weaponization of space, should Canada join.

Most importantly for opponents of Canadian participation in missile defence, the issue now has the potential to become a federal election issue, given recent developments and the New Democratic Party's focus on missile defence. The NDP sees missile defence as a wedge issue, and the government's policy changes can be interpreted as evidence that the government feels vulnerable on this issue.

At no other time in the history of this issue in Canada has the opportunity to achieve a victory over missile defence been greater than in the coming eight months.

However, without a concerted effort by civil society organizations to keep the issue before Canadians and to voice the widespread concern about Canada's moves toward the Bush administration, the opportunity could be lost.

A Canada-wide strategy to inform the work of organization and activists is needed, and where possible, joint efforts will maximize impact on the public debate.

Goal:
To prevent Canadian participation in missile defence by effectively conveying opposition from a broad spectrum of civil society

Objectives:
1. To write, release at a press conference and publicize in the media an open letter endorsed by Canadians of national prominence by mid-March.
2. To create a coalition of organizations and individuals from across Canada opposing missile defence.
3. To place missile defence clearly on the agenda of candidates and politicians over the pre-election, election, and post-election period.
4. To build Canadian opposition to missile defence through the sharing and dissemination of resources, exchange of information, coordination of certain activities, and the development of resources, including a Web site.
5. To assist international efforts in opposition to missile

defence through international coordination with partners and networks.

Structure of Coalition:

The Coalition is open to any groups which endorse the goal and objectives of the Coalition. A running list of members will be maintained on a Web site.

In the weeks that followed, dozens of organizations added their names to the coalition. Later, we substituted the word "Campaign" for "Coalition" to better describe a more informal, action-oriented organization, and became the Canadian Campaign to Oppose Missile Defence. But this name was really only used amongst ourselves, since we decided early on that we would conduct our work under the name of our individual organizations and affiliations, rather than trying to build an identity for yet another organization.

We received a start-up grant from the Vancouver-based Simons Foundation, which supports many disarmament initiatives, and with this financial support in hand, Debbie and I conducted a search and hired Sara Kemp as our campaign coordinator. A recent graduate of Carleton University, specializing in international affairs, Sara was also an experienced student organizer. She would work out of the Polaris Institute's modest office in downtown Ottawa and become an integral part of the campaign.

* * *

There is a running joke among activists that, whenever something mysterious happens with their phone system, it's because Canada's spy agency, CSIS, is tapping the call. Hear strange clinking sounds or your line is disconnecting for no apparent reason? It must be CSIS. In fact, if you were to ask any person working on issues like missile defence, they would tell you that they conduct their business with the assumption that CSIS *is* listening in on their calls. My guess is that they secretly hope that CSIS is listening, just to validate their feeling that their work is "dangerous" for the government and the "powers that be."

I have really never worried about being spied upon. That's why I was very surprised when I received a call from a real CSIS agent.

The agent first left me a message asking me to return her call. She gave her direct line, which perhaps was redirected to a cell phone, and when she spoke to me she asked for a meeting to discuss an investigation she was conducting on someone. She repeatedly assured me the investigation had nothing to do with me personally, but was looking at someone from one of the Ottawa embassies whom I knew.

I asked for a name, and she told me it was someone at the Russian embassy. She said that they review all new appointments of foreign officials to Canada, and that this man's activities were leading them to believe he was involved in work beyond the scope of his diplomatic posting. I guess that was technical language to suggest that they thought he was a spy. They wanted to ask me a few questions about his behaviour and any requests he may have made.

A word of explanation: when I began work on security issues in Ottawa and had a few articles appear here and there, I began to receive calls from staff members of the foreign embassies in town. These folks were mostly analysts and researchers who wanted to chat about defence policy or missile defence or other related topics. I figured it was part of their job to be in touch with "experts" outside of the government, and so I always made time to chat. Besides, you never know what you may learn.

In addition to meeting with Romanians, Taiwanese, and others, I had had lunch occasionally with this man from the Russian embassy. He was a young Russian foreign-service officer who had recently been posted to Canada. We met every few months, usually at his invitation, to chat about missile defence, Russia, Canada, and the state of the world generally.

I always assumed that his interest in missile defence stemmed from the fact of who his boss was here in Ottawa. The Russian ambassador to Canada is Georgiy Mamedov, a former Russian arms-control negotiator between Russia and the United States. Mamedov is also a critic of George W. Bush's missile-defence program, because of its potential implications for the development of space weapons and the risk of a new nuclear-arms race. Mamedov waded into the debate in 2004 when he told the *Globe and Mail* that Pentagon briefings he had received showed that missile defence would ultimately involve space weapons.

I was startled by the CSIS request for a meeting, and did not agree to it right away. Instead, I said I would call them back after I had had time to consider their request. The agent said she would be joined by another agent, a specialist responsible for the investigation, and suggested that the meeting could be held either at our downtown office or at CSIS headquarters in the east end of Ottawa, whichever we preferred.

I think the agent was surprised by my reluctance to agree to a meeting, but the idea of meeting with CSIS left me a bit uncomfortable. This was not because of who they are or what they do—there are some good reasons to have an intelligence-gathering agency such as theirs. But most of all I did not want to become *involved* with CSIS. For example, I didn't want to enter unwittingly into any unwritten agreements or understandings with them, or worse, have my information result in some erroneous conclusions about my Russian acquaintance.

The last time I had had lunch with him was about a week before the call from CSIS. We had eaten at the Mayflower restaurant on Elgin Street and had chatted about missile defence, politics in Canada, his work at the embassy, which includes preparing for various Russian delegations coming to Canada, even about our summer vacations. Pretty innocuous stuff.

I concluded that CSIS must have been following him that day. They probably tailed him to my office, and then followed us to the restaurant, perhaps taking photos of me for identification later. It would be as easy as looking on the Internet to figure out who I was; my photo and contact number are on our Web site. But the thought of being followed and photographed was disconcerting.

I talked it over with Tony Clarke and my lawyer colleague Steven Shrybman, who also put me in touch with Paul Copeland, an expert on CSIS. Finally I agreed to the meeting with CSIS on two conditions: one, that Tony would also be present, and two, that I could tape record the conversation.

Well, the agent certainly did not like the idea of the conversation being recorded. I could almost hear her grimace at that suggestion over the phone, but this issue was set aside as we discussed where the meeting would be held. Tony and I had decided we should meet at their office, so that's what I suggested to the agent. She agreed and gave me detailed information about how to get into the building: enter this gate, go to that guardhouse, present your photo ID, you'll be on the list, etc. We determined a date and time to meet; everything was set.

But then came the punch line.

"One more thing," she said just as we were about to hang up, "You're not allowed to bring tape recorders into the building."

"Oh..." I replied. "Well then, we'll have to meet at our office."

The whole tape-recorder issue may seem to have been a petty concern on my part, but my intention was not so much to keep a record of the meeting as to ensure that the conduct of the meeting was "straight up" and on the record. The last thing I wanted was for one of the agents to tell me something about my Russian acquaintance and then say, "Oh, but you can't tell him that secret information." As I said, I did not want to enter into any "understanding" with CSIS, and the fact that they were so resistant to being recorded seemed to validate my concerns.

The day of the meeting arrived, and the two agents met with Tony and me at our small office on Cooper Street in downtown Ottawa. We began with polite chit-chat, but then it came time to start the meeting. "As I mentioned, I would like this conversation to be 'on the record,' and I will record the conversation if there are no objections," I said, as I put the small tape recorder on the table next to my notepad. I didn't turn it on.

The CSIS special investigator appeared to become very agitated. For several minutes he queried me: why did I want the meeting recorded, what would the tape be used for, would it be given to the subject of the investigation? I replied that I was participating in the interview to assist them with carrying out their legitimate inquiries, and the recording would remain in my own possession.

But he couldn't get past the issue. He lashed out, "Let me get this straight: you meet with a foreign government and don't record the conversation, but you insist on recording a conversation with your own government?"

"Look, we've spent ten minutes on this," I said, trying to defuse the situation. "Let's just get on with it." And I turned on the recorder.

During the interview the investigator asked me about my meetings with the Russian, what we generally discussed, whether he seemed to be pushing for information or names of decision-makers in the government, and whether at any point I felt uncomfortable with any of his requests. My responses were that we had only met a couple of times, the conversations were general, and he seemed mostly interested in learning about my views on the missile-defence issue, and not much more. The interview ended after only a few minutes, and I turned off the recorder.

The agents seemed satisfied with the meeting, and explained that it was their job to ensure that all representatives of foreign governments behave appropriately. Tony and I nodded and agreed that they had an important role to play.

Then Tony asked them, "So, you need to monitor all of the embassies in town. Do you have someone watching the U.S. embassy?"

The agents chuckled. "Oh no, they're our friends," he said. We all shared a good laugh.

To this day I haven't mentioned any of this to my Russian acquaintance, even though we have continued to meet for lunch occasionally. What would I say? "Oh, by the way, CSIS is following you. Pass the salt?" I figure that, like my activists friends in Canada, he operates assuming he is being monitored by the Canadian authorities. It comes with the job.

The idea that a Russian agent would be able to get useful information from me is really laughable. I have no access to government secrets. I read the same newspapers as everybody else. In retrospect, I think that CSIS did not want to know if I was spying, even unwittingly, for the Russians. On the contrary, they were probably more interested in learning if I would spy on the Russians for CSIS. Who knows how the conversation would have gone had I not insisted on tape-recording it?

A few months after our meeting with CSIS, I was called by a reporter who asked me to comment on a report he had received from CSIS through an "access to information" request. The report was written in January 2005 and was entitled, "The Creation of a New Peace Movement?"

The report examined the evolution of the anti-globalization movement into a peace movement, and CSIS had obviously been keeping tabs on the various groups involved in the campaign. The report, marked "Secret," noted that "Canadian peace activists also hope to take advantage of the current collective mobilization against the war in Iraq to organize major demonstrations against the American missile defense project." The next sentence was censored.

4

MAKING AN IMPACT ON OTTAWA

Throughout the 1990s, social movements became very disengaged from parliamentary politics. But in the world after September 11, 2001, when national governments were once again asserting their power, we needed to find a way to re-engage with governments and parliamentary politics. This required experimenting with different approaches, including finding ways to work with the political parties. This did not mean hitching our wagon to a single party, but in some cases it required working *with* parties, *between* parties, and even *within* parties.

For instance, it made sense that the NDP would be the best place to start when we were putting our campaign together in early 2004, since it was strongly opposed to missile defence, and traditionally has had the closest links with groups like ours outside of parliament. As the campaign evolved, the NDP became an important part of our political strategy.

In addition to the NDP, we had built a good working relationship with the Bloc Québécois, the other party opposed to missile defence. Since the Bloc was a party based in Quebec and our campaign largely worked in English Canada, however, it meant that our interests didn't align as closely as they did with the NDP, but we shared information and analysis.

Even in the case of the Liberals, there were many MPs who shared our concerns and did not want Canada to join the U.S. program.

Traditionally, these left-leaning Liberals have been referred to as "social Liberals," in contrast to the more conservative members who are known as "business Liberals" (Prime Minister Paul Martin was a member of the latter). We could work with many social Liberals on influencing the government's policy.

As the campaign progressed, we even found a few within the Conservative Party who wanted to keep Canada out of the U.S. missile-defence program. Despite being an "endangered political species," there are still a few "Red Tories" in Ottawa.

When the 2004 election resulted in a minority Liberal government, having connections in all the parties would become very important and gave our campaign tremendous leverage in Ottawa. Every single MP's vote became an issue of political life or death for Paul Martin's government, and none could be taken for granted. By pulling support away from his position in favour of missile defence either in the opposition parties or in his own Liberal Party, we dramatically increased the likelihood of winning.

* * *

"You're going to like what Jack is coming out with," Jamey Heath said to me when we passed each other on a busy downtown Ottawa street. It was the summer of 2002, and Jamey was heading up the NDP leadership campaign of a city councillor from Toronto by the name of Jack Layton.

I knew Jamey as a good campaigner, who had worked inside the NDP, the Canadian Union of Public Employees, and even Greenpeace. In 1997 he had run for office in Ottawa Centre against Liberal incumbent Mac Harb, placing a strong second. Jamey has had unique experience, having worked in three of the communities that largely comprise "the Left" in Canada: the NDP, labour unions, and activist groups.

So it made sense that Jamey ended up working with Jack Layton. From his reputation, it appeared that Jack saw himself first as a social activist and environmentalist, and took up politics mostly to advance his activist ideals. For me, this set Jack Layton apart from many people I was accustomed to working with over the years in the NDP—people who seemed much less comfortable as activists than as politicians.

I had kept in touch with Jamey on various issues that I was working on, especially military spending and other peace and disarmament issues. I had been trying to convince Jamey, and through him Jack, that Canada's spending was very high, despite what the newspapers said, and there was a strong case to call for a freeze on Canadian military spending. I presumed from Jamey's comment that Jack was going to adopt that position as well.

A few weeks after my encounter with Jamey, I received a copy of a leaflet from Jack Layton's NDP leadership campaign. It took very strong and positive positions on peace issues, including calling for a freeze on military spending. Jamey was right; I thought it was terrific. I felt it showed that Jack was not afraid to show leadership on these issues.

From reading his materials and hearing him speak at one or two NDP events, it was clear to me that Jack was very comfortable working within the same social movements that I had been involved in for many years. While there have been some links between the NDP and social movements, my impression was that, if he won his campaign for party leader, Jack would lead the NDP to embrace this relationship with greater enthusiasm than in the past. Jack was riding on a growing feeling within the NDP that the party needed to renew its links with its roots, and with the broader social movements that were challenging economic globalization so forcefully. One group that advocated this new approach for the NDP was the New Politics Initiative.

The NPI was composed of NDP members (and others), including Jim Stanford from the Canadian Auto Workers, author and activist Judy Rebick (who always reminded people that she was not an NDP member), and my good friend author Murray Dobbin. The group argued that the NDP should forge strong links with social movements, such as the anti-globalization movement (sometimes more precisely called the anti-corporate-globalization movement to avoid creating the false impression that it is protectionist or nationalist), the women's movement, the environmental movement, and the peace movement.

The NPI vision statement argued that strengthening ties between parliamentary and extra-parliamentary groups was crucial for the

NDP's future success—even if it required dissolving the party and starting anew. The NPI's leaders saw the future of the NDP, or a new party,
in the young faces of those protesting globalization. The party had to
become connected with the new youth movement that had been born
in November 1999: the movement had taken on the World Trade
Organization in Seattle and had successfully derailed the global free-
trade meeting in the now famous "Battle of Seattle."

Jack Layton never formally joined the NPI, but NDP MPs Libby
Davies and Svend Robinson from Vancouver, both leaders of the NPI,
endorsed Layton's leadership bid. A more conservative group within
the NDP backed Layton's main rival, NDP MP Bill Blaikie from
Winnipeg. Thus the NDP leadership campaign essentially boiled down
to new school vs. old school.

In late 2002, Jack Layton, with his new dynamic style and media
flair, won the endorsement of former party leader Ed Broadbent. To
many NDP members, Broadbent's endorsement signalled that Jack
Layton was acceptable, even endorsed by the party elite. Jack Layton
won the leadership of the NDP in January 2003.

* * *

A few weeks after Jack Layton had moved from Toronto to Ottawa as
NDP Leader, Tony Clarke and I were laying out our plans for the coming few months.

"Tony, we should set up a meeting with Jack Layton after he's settled
in," I suggested.

"Yeah, that's a good idea," Tony replied. "And let's not go in with a
set agenda. It would be good to just talk informally, explain our programs broadly, and explore where there might be opportunities to
come together."

It may sound like nothing more than a simple meeting of like-
minded people, but it was significant. The truth was, by then I had
been in Ottawa for three years working on national issues and had had
little direct interaction with the political life of Parliament Hill—and
almost no contact with the NDP. You might expect that someone who
had been working at Canada's largest and most successful citizen

organization, the Council of Canadians, as I had, would have been on the Hill all the time. But that wasn't the case.

In fact, it wasn't unusual for Ottawa activist organizations to have little contact with the political process, or the NDP, because many groups felt that the corporations had taken over the political direction of the country. During the 1990s, "corporate rule" became the predominant understanding of politics in Canada amongst many progressives who saw the government as essentially powerless, which obviously put lobbying the government far down the list of campaign priorities. Governments became seemingly powerless, as free enterprise and private interests overcame any notion of the public interest and the positive role governments could play in society.

The idea that big business was running the country from behind the scenes had been reinforced as one pro-business policy after another, generated by business-funded think-tanks, became official government policy. One of the most successful of these big-business groups was Tom d'Aquino's Business Council on National Issues (BCNI), now the Canadian Council of Chief Executives (CCCE). The BCNI championed the Canada–U.S. free-trade agreement under Brian Mulroney and then the North American Free Trade agreement under Jean Chrétien, followed by years of draconian spending cuts on social programs, generous tax cuts, and wholesale privatization of government services.

The Polaris Institute was founded to help social movements develop strategies to address "corporate rule." The Polaris Institute's founder and director, Tony Clarke, describes the institute on its Web site:

> The term polaris itself refers to the original Greek word for the north star. Just as ships lost at sea have often turned to the north star to guide them home, the Polaris Institute tries to provide a compass for social movements in this new age of corporate-driven globalization. The prime objective of Polaris is to guide people "home" to the essence of democracy and their role as citizens. The task is to assist citizen movements in developing campaign strategies for democratic social change by targeting and confronting the corporate powers that have

hijacked the public policy making process at local, national
and international levels. Thus, the north star in our logo serves
as an ecological symbol for our role as a compass for social
movements.

Tony described his evolution in thinking about the changing nature
of power in his 1997 book, *Silent Coup: Confronting the Big Business
Takeover of Canada*. He emphasized the need for social movements to
retool for the new political reality, which was ushered in by Brian
Mulroney's Conservatives and then implemented by Jean Chrétien's
Liberals.

> Between 1987 and 1993, one of the largest social movements
> ever assembled in this country came together to fight [the free
> trade] battle. We knew full well that the Business Council on
> National Issues, composed of the largest domestic and for-
> eign-owned corporations in Canada, had been the driving
> force behind the free trade deal with the U.S. We even labelled
> it the "corporate agenda" in our campaigns. But our strategies
> and tactics did not measure up to our analysis ...

> While we managed to force a national election on the issue in
> 1988, and even turned public opinion around to the point
> where the majority of Canadians voted against free trade, the
> Mulroney Conservatives still swept back into power ... When
> the Liberals took over Parliament Hill by storm in the 1993
> election ... they immediately abandoned their long-standing
> opposition to the Mulroney free trade agenda ... In effect, the
> corporate agenda was alive and well in Ottawa, with the
> Business Council of National Issues still firmly in the driver's
> seat.

> As I reflected on these and related developments, it became
> more and more clear that, as a country, we were moving into a
> new political era in the twilight years of the 20th century. To

be sure, corporations, both Canadian-based and foreign-owned, have always played a powerful role in shaping public policy directions in Canada. But in the new global economy, free trade agreements like NAFTA had become nothing less than charters of rights and freedoms for transnational corporations ...

In short, we are now living in a new political era of corporate rule. Moreover, these new political realities, in turn, have profound implications for the model and strategies used by citizens' movements to bring about democratic social change.

Tony's book was seminal, and provided the analytical framework for the burgeoning anti-globalization movement, which went on to defeat such global free-trade initiatives as the Multilateral Agreement on Investment (MAI) in 1998 and the Seattle Round of the WTO in 1999. Today, the prevalence of corporate rule is a commonly accepted and widely understood concept, which has guided much of the thinking and strategies of the movement. Take a look at any of the popular books in this subject area, such as Naomi Klein's bestseller *No Logo*, and you can see how "corporate rule" has influenced many writers and thinkers.

But not everyone embraced the idea of corporate rule and the impotence of governments. People working within political parties felt that social movements were undervaluing the world of progressive parliamentarians.

Svend Robinson, NDP member of parliament for Burnaby Douglas, saw himself as an activist like any other. In 2001 he had asked to be allowed to sit as a representative of the NDP on a coalition of non-governmental organizations and trade unions opposed to the World Trade Organization called the Common Front on the WTO. Saying he didn't want the party to have "a seat at the back of the bus," he sought a status for the NDP equal to that of the non-governmental groups and labour unions.

During the discussion at the coalition meeting, representatives of the Council of Canadians, myself included, argued that the NDP should attend as an observer but not as a member equal to the other groups. For example, the NDP should not be able to speak for the coalition at a press conference.

If the media and the public saw that there were many different voices speaking out on our issues outside parliament, this helped the NDP inside parliament much more than if the NDP was officially connected with social movement organizations.

The groups agreed that there needed to be a distinction between the coalition and political parties. Although he was welcome to attend the meetings as an observer, Svend left without his seat at the table.

Svend's rebuff likely confirmed the attitude of some of his NDP colleagues who did not share his views about working so closely with social movements. They would argue that the NDP has to win votes, and social movements don't deliver them. Non-governmental organizations, many of which receive government grants and want to stay in the good graces of the governing party, will not risk their funding by encouraging their members and supporters to vote for the NDP.

The frustration amongst some NDP MPs with social movements that overlooked parliamentary politics in their campaigns was evident in a speech given by MP Bill Blaikie while on the hustings for the NDP leadership. Bill was Jack Layton's main rival, and during his speech at an NDP barbecue I attended during the summer of 2002, Bill reminded the crowd that the activists who claimed victory for defeating the notorious international-trade agreement, the Multilateral Agreement on Investment, overlooked the fact that it was a decision by a government—in this case the French government—that ultimately killed the deal.

But by the time that Jack Layton became leader of the NDP in January 2003, the political chess table had changed significantly, and it seemed that parliamentary politics was once again an arena to which social movements needed to pay more attention.

Since the terrorist attacks of September 11, 2001, the world has witnessed a resurgence of the power of the state, especially in matters of security. As U.S. leaders like to point out to Canadians, "security trumps trade" these days, and security can only be delivered by the state—not corporations. As Maude Barlow put it, "governments matter again."

In addition, Jean Chrétien's iron grip on parliament and the Liberal Party was over, and Paul Martin, who had pledged to address the "democratic deficit," had just taken power.

Finally, the anti-corporate-globalization movement was in decline, arguably because its analysis and tactics could not make the shift to the post-September 11, 2001, political environment, and a new movement opposed to the Bush administration and the invasion of Iraq was sending hundreds of thousands of people opposed to the U.S. invasion of Iraq into the Canadian streets.

With Jack's election as NDP leader, I felt that we could revisit the question: how should social movements deal with the Canadian political system?

That's why I suggested to Tony we meet with Jack, taking him up on his openness to collaboration between parliamentary and extra-parliamentary groups. The Polaris Institute could act as that "north star" Tony referred to by helping social movements sort through the current political moment, especially in light of the new NDP leadership.

* * *

In February 2003, Tony and I, along with several other members of our staff, made the trip to NDP headquarters in a downtown office tower. Normally meetings of this nature would be held in the parliament building itself, but Jack had yet to win a seat in parliament, so his office wasn't yet on the Hill

The meeting went very well; it was a good exchange of information and ideas. We could already see Jack's ideas at work in how the NDP was reorganizing itself. He had asked his long-time executive assistant, Franz Hartmann, to work directly with NGOs and to build bridges between social movements and the party.

Jack and Franz said they wanted to choose two or three "campaigns" for the NDP to focus on. They weren't talking about election campaigns, but issue campaigns: climate change, peace, public health care.

As well, they wanted to increase the capacity of their local NDP riding associations to function as campaigning, activist groups. This would be an important change in the role of riding associations, since they typically function only to raise money and help out at election time. A few months later the party launched its own Star Wars campaign which was directed at enlivening the party's grassroots and educating the general public about the issue.

They also had plans to set up "advocacy teams" that would be led by NDP members of parliament and would include members of activist groups and research organizations. For instance, Alexa McDonough, the MP for Halifax, would regularly bring together peace activists and experts in her capacity as the foreign-affairs critic. Later, Alexa did exactly that, and her advocacy team, comprising both NDP party members and staff along with citizen groups, produced some of the best strategic thinking and political analysis of the entire anti-missile defence campaign.

Tony and I were impressed. Coming away from the meeting, we could both see some potential in addressing the chasm that had developed between social movements and parliamentary politics. The advocacy teams could be a good first step for groups to connect, or in some cases reconnect, with the NDP. And if the riding associations were successfully encouraged to take up issue campaigns between elections, this could strengthen the connection between activist groups and the NDP at the local level.

The strategy put forward at the meeting was not unlike the kind of planning we do in activist organizations. "Listening to the way Jack and Franz were talking about issue campaign strategy, I felt as if I were in a meeting back at the Council of Canadians," I said to Tony as we walked back to our office.

* * *

"The prime minister's office is receiving an anti-missile-defence e-mail three times a minute—that's one every twenty seconds," I said over the phone to my colleague Peter Coombes in Vancouver. Peter was the former coordinator of the Vancouver peace group End the Arms Race, and in the early 1990s he had given me my first job after I moved to the West Coast from Fredericton. We have worked together in one way or another ever since, and our latest project was a Web site called Ceasefire.ca that used the Internet as a means to lobby the government.

By late March 2004, thousands of people were signing the "Stars Against Star Wars" letter we had launched only a few days before at our poorly attended press conference in Toronto.

We had posted the letter on Ceasefire.ca, and invited our supporters to add their names and to encourage others to do the same. As mentioned, each time a person signed their name over the Internet, they also sent a copy of the letter to the prime minister's office in Ottawa.

"Today we'll break all of our previous records on Ceasefire.ca. Looks like more than fifteen hundred letters will be sent before the end of the day," I said.

"If that doesn't send the message that Canadians don't want to join that thing, I don't know what will," Peter replied.

By the end of the campaign, more than fifty thousand letters opposed to missile defence had been sent to Ottawa through Ceasefire.ca. Today's activist has gained a powerful organizing tool—the Internet. The use of e-mails, Web sites, and other applications allows activists to stay in touch almost constantly.

If an official makes a comment about missile defence and it is reported on a news-media Web site, thousands of activists will know what he said within hours—sometimes minutes—as word spreads through a mass-distributed e-mail message. The e-mail is then forwarded again and again to sub-networks of people, branching out exponentially from the original list of recipients. The first e-mail will then spur more e-mail exchanges, as people discuss the development, and often experts will provide analysis and commentary. All this will flash across activists' computer screens across the country or around the world, nearly simultaneously.

The widespread use of the Internet by activists was first widely recognized during the large, anti-globalization demonstrations outside the meeting of the WTO in Seattle in 1999. CNN, reporting on the phenomenon, quoted one of the protest organizers:

"Information is power, as governments and companies have long realized, and that's why they have tried to control access to information," said Charles Secrett, London director of Friends of the Earth, the environmental group. "What the Internet does is that it makes information available to everybody, quickly and relatively cheaply," Secrett said. "And that is an enormous tool for citizen activism. We saw that at the World Trade Organization meeting in Seattle. So we think it's a fantastic and vital democratic tool."

In 1999, I had been a regional organizer for the Council of Canadians in Vancouver, the organization's first office outside national headquarters in Ottawa. I was deeply involved in organizing the thousands of Canadians who travelled to Seattle for the WTO demonstrations. One of my strongest memories is standing at the Canada–U.S. border just after sunrise on November 29, 1999, as our forty-one buses full of people were lined up as far down the road as I could see, waiting to be cleared and to carry on to Seattle for the big demonstrations.

Since those days, the Internet has grown to such widespread use that networks of activists use e-mail and Web sites as their main form of communication. I use the word "networks" rather than "organizations," because the Internet has not only changed communication, it has also changed organizing.

Most people who are engaged in social movements today, especially young people, would never join an organization. The idea of signing a membership card, paying a fee, receiving a monthly newsletter in their mailbox, or attending a meeting on the first Wednesday evening of every month is absolutely foreign to their experience.

In fact, many young people reject the notion of "leadership" altogether. To some, calling someone a leader is an insult. They view their networks as politically flat and operate by consensus. Group decisions are still made in meetings, often held in university classrooms, trade-union meeting rooms, or in church basements, but the bulk of the information-sharing and organizing occurs over the Internet. Of course, there are de facto leaders, but they generally assume that role based on their skills, experience, influence, and networking ability, not through anything akin to an election.

It is ironic that the Internet, which is used by anti-war activists, was originally constructed by the U.S. military. The electronic system of communication was intended to allow military forces on the East Coast to communicate with the West Coast in the event of a nuclear attack. E-mail messages find their way to their intended recipient like a mouse going through a maze; if one route is blocked, it will try another. The system would therefore allow messages to traverse the continental United States, even if much of the network (and the United States itself) were destroyed by nuclear explosions.

A year before our missile-defence campaign began in earnest, Peter Coombes, Jillian Skeet, and I were very concerned about the low level of activity among citizen groups in light of the missile discussions that had been initiated in May of that year. My challenge was that the Polaris Institute was primarily an action-research body and not a constituency-based organization with a membership that could be called upon for campaigns. So we applied the lessons we had learned about Internet organizing to establish our Web site, Ceasefire.ca, whose mission was "to provide people with Web-based tools to take political action and promote peace, disarmament, and social justice."

The Web site essentially provided a means for the average person to write a letter about missile defence, or choose a pre-written letter, and e-mail it to the government. Using computer programming by two long-time friends who had their own Internet company, Loc Dao and Lara Kroeker, we were able to build a list of contact information for people who indicated that they wished to be e-mailed about future actions or campaign developments.

When we launched the site in June 2003, we sent our first e-mail to a few hundred friends and contacts, encouraging them to come to the Ceasefire.ca Web site and send that letter to then-prime minister Jean Chrétien against missile defence. The list grew as word spread over the Internet about Ceasefire.ca, mostly because of people who had sent a letter, then sent a note to ten of their friends telling them about the Web site and the issue, which was one of the options we offered. They in turn came to the site, sent their own letter, and told ten more friends. Our list of contacts grew exponentially, and a few hundred names quickly expanded to many thousands within a year.

To draw even more attention to the issue, and Ceasefire.ca, we asked well-known Canadians to actually write a letter that we could e-mail to our supporters, educating them about missile defence and encouraging them to send a letter to the government. Soon we were sending letters to our contact list from Mel Watkins, Maude Barlow, David Suzuki, Mel Hurtig, Helen Caldicott, and even former California senator, 1960s radical, and former husband of Jane Fonda, Tom Hayden.

We received a special boost from Canadian musician Matthew Good, who took our materials on tour with him across Canada and encouraged his audiences to go to Ceasefire.ca and contact the government about missile defence. During my travels I met many young people who had attended one of Matt's concerts and as result became active in the campaign.

On several occasions during the campaign, we had concrete evidence that the flood of e-mails being sent to the government by Canadians was having an impact. In the fall of 2004 we initiated a letter-writing campaign on Ceasefire.ca to members of the Commons Foreign Affairs Committee (which was an all-party committee) calling for public hearings on missile defence.

We didn't get our hearings, but the MPs felt our presence. Conservative MP Kevin Sorenson said he had been inundated with hundreds of e-mails demanding public hearings.

While the Conservative member complained about receiving e-mails, other MPs felt quite the opposite. One of our e-mail campaigns sent letters of encouragement to Liberal MPs who were opposed to missile defence, despite Paul Martin's professed support for the idea. Hundreds of e-mails of support were sent to these MPs from voters across the country. Word must have been spreading in the hallways of Parliament Hill, because one day a Liberal backbencher phoned us and said, "Please add me to your Web site; I'm against missile defence too!"

* * *

In early April 2004, Sara Kemp and I were meeting daily in my office, assessing where we should focus our energy for the election campaign itself, which was expected to be called in the next few weeks.

"People I'm talking to across the country generally feel the need to be a part of something larger," Sara said. "I think that's what the campaign can offer. People are looking for campaign materials, especially information brochures and placards. They want information on how to organize events such as all-candidates forums, and they just want to hear what other organizations are doing."

Our slow start with the modest launch of our missile-defence letter back in March began to snowball into an avalanche in the weeks before the election, which would eventually be called for June 28, 2004. We hoped that the flurry of activities—e-mails, letters, op-eds, public meetings—was beginning to shift public opinion from neutrality on missile defence to opposition.

The government must have been feeling the impact of the campaign too. Despite the fact that the prime minister had publicly stated his support for joining the U.S. missile shield, and that he had appointed the hawkish David Pratt as defence minister to steer the negotiations with the United States, the Liberals delayed making a decision on whether or not to join until after the election. One unnamed Liberal official was quoted as saying, "Missile defence is a vote-loser for us." We saw this as a small-but-encouraging victory for the campaign.

As the election approached, we broke our strategy down into three sets of objectives: political, communications, and organizing.

Political objectives: Promote missile defence as an election issue by encouraging debate among parties and candidates on missile defence, facilitate public queries of candidates on the issue, and make the media aware of the public's interest in the issue.

Communications objectives: Encourage journalists covering Paul Martin to ask him to comment on missile defence issues and development. Develop relationships with journalists assigned to cover Paul Martin during the election and focus media actions on them.

Organizing objectives: Structure the campaign to allow the broadest possible participation. Be non-partisan, open to individuals or groups, and as informal as possible to ensure participation from established and ad hoc organizations.

We developed an idea that we felt would support our objectives for the election campaign; we called it "rapid-response teams." The assumption was that there would be a group of journalists covering Paul Martin all the time, travelling with him on the campaign airplane and taking the Martin bus to all of his campaign stops. We wanted to keep the missile-defence issue before them at all times.

With this in mind, we thought we could take advantage of the Canada-wide network we had developed by identifying a small team of people in every city to stage small protests with anti-missile-defence placards and leaflets at Paul Martin's campaign stops. Sara would monitor the media to track Martin's scheduled stops, and then use the Internet to alert the rapid-response team in each city. The team would need to be prepared to react quickly to Sara's alert, because she would likely have less than twenty-four hours' notice of his stops. While each protest would be small, they would be repeated over and over again wherever the prime minister went. The theory was that the repetition of smaller actions would be as effective as a single large demonstration (which we were unsure we could pull off).

On May 23, 2004, Prime Minister Martin called the federal election for June 28, and we were ready. Sara had organized twenty-three rapid-response teams across the country. We had produced new leaflets, organizing tips, and talking points for our activists to use. Missile defence was going to be an election issue, and we would do our best to keep it visible in the media.

Two days into the election, Paul Martin visited Charlottetown, and our rapid-response team, led by Leo Broderick of the Council of Canadians, was ready for him. The team had made placards decrying missile defence and the Bush Star Wars scheme, and were at Martin's scheduled stop an hour before he arrived at Province House, where the fathers of Confederation had met. When Martin appeared, he was confronted by the team's twenty-five members, holding signs and chanting "No Star Wars." As we had hoped, the media picked up on the team's message and the protest was included in national TV coverage that night, and in many newspapers.

Sara spent the next few weeks mobilizing our rapid-reaction teams. Local activists "bird dogged" Paul Martin across the country. In Victoria, a group of activists met Martin's plane with umbrellas that read "missile defence—no way." Later that same day, Martin was confronted by our rapid-response team at a Liberal rally in Surrey, a Vancouver suburb. By the time he landed in Edmonton later that week, members of our rapid-response team reported that Martin had a distinct sneer when they showed up with their signs.

The project was a great success. It put pressure on Paul Martin, supported our media work, and helped involve the people on the ground who had become part of the campaign. I learned an important lesson: our campaign was most effective when our three strategies—political, communications, and organizing—worked together at the same time. From that point on, I also looked for the right moment when we could put pressure on the government by working through the media and utilizing our grassroots base in communities across the country.

As the campaign progressed the feedback we were receiving from groups on the ground indicated they wanted to put together a "day of action." A day of action occurs when people in numerous communities stage protests making the same demand of the government on the same day. We had a conference call with dozens of activists from all regions, and June 12, 2004, was chosen for our "Cross-Canada Wake-Up Call on Missile Defence."

A dozen cities held small demonstrations that day. In Ottawa, we picked a street corner on Bank Street and we invited all the candidates who were running in the Ottawa area to come downtown and sign a pledge that said, "I Won't Vote for Missile Defence." Several NDP candidates, a Green Party candidate, and other candidates signed our pledge. The best-known candidate was Monia Mazigh, the wife of Maher Arar, who was running for the NDP in Ottawa South.

The Raging Grannies were there as well, that well-known group of senior citizens who don their shawls and Easter bonnets and sing their anti-war songs (usually familiar melodies with newly written, politically sharp lyrics). This time the Grannies brought alarm clocks for a "missile defence wake-up call." All the clocks went off at the same time. It made for a good local story on TV that night. The candidates had their moment on camera, and the ringing alarm clocks were an effective gimmick.

Later in the election campaign, rather than have our teams sit around waiting for Paul Martin to arrive in their hometowns, we encouraged actions outside all the political leaders' campaign rallies and photo-ops. Of course the demonstrations around Jack Layton's campaign had a more supportive flavour, since he was adamantly opposed to Star Wars.

By the time Canadians cast their ballots on June 28, I was very pleased with the actions we had managed to muster during the election campaign. The missile-defence issue was always seen by journalists as one of the top election issues, and it did feature prominently in the televised debates and during interviews with the party leaders. But to be honest, the issue did not catch fire as I had hoped it would, despite our best efforts. Even when the Liberals' polling numbers were slipping downward at the end of the campaign, Paul Martin did not reach for the issue. Instead, he decided to create a panic amongst moderate voters by accusing Stephen Harper's Conservatives of having a hidden, socially conservative agenda.

I can only assume that his polling numbers were telling him that missile defence was not a "ballot question." A ballot question is one that is in the voter's mind as he or she is standing in the polling booth, and is the main determining factor in who receives his or her vote. For example, in the last U.S. election, gay marriage was a ballot issue in many Southern states. Voters were asked if they supported gay marriage on the same ballot as the one on which they were asked to choose a president. Religious and conservative voters went to the polls to vote against gay marriage, and then ticked off a vote for George W. Bush. Had the gay-marriage issue not been included on the ballot, it's likely that far fewer people would have voted, and Bush would have received fewer votes than he did.

Instead of pushing missile defence as a ballot question, the Liberal strategists wanted to portray Stephen Harper and his Conservative Party as having a secret agenda to impose their socially conservative values on Canadians, particularly gay marriage and possibly even a woman's right to have an abortion. Some of Harper's own candidates, one of whom made some revealing remarks about using the Constitution's notwithstanding clause to prevent legalized gay marriage, handed Liberal strategists enough evidence to convince moderate, urban voters that voting for the Liberals would be a vote against Harper's secret agenda.

Moreover, the Liberals have a tradition of "campaigning from the Left, and governing from the Right." By sounding like a progressive, left-leaning party during an election campaign, the Liberals portray themselves as being essentially the same as the NDP, influencing many of the urban-based, moderate, socially conscious voters to support Liberal candidates at the expense of the NDP.

A good example of this was the Liberal Red Book of campaign promises in the 1993 election, which read like the NDP's platform. But once in office, the party dropped its opposition to free trade and brought in NAFTA, and in then Finance Minister Paul Martin's infamous 1995 budget slashed billions of dollars from social programs.

The polls showed the Liberals and the Conservatives in a virtual dead heat right up to the final days of the campaign, so the Liberals pushed the "Stephen Harper is scary" envelope as far as it would go. Realizing that many of the votes they had counted on winning were moving to the Liberals, Jack pleaded with voters to "give the NDP a strong voice in Parliament," as he said in speech after speech.

By the last week before the election, the polls showed the Liberals had managed to regain lost ground and had a small lead over the Conservatives. Many of the last-minute votes that went to the Liberals were drawn from the NDP, and this hurt the party in many ridings. In about a dozen close races, the NDP candidate lost by less than a thousand votes. On election day, NDP hopes of winning up to 40 seats in the 308-seat House of Commons were dashed when the party won only 19 seats. While still an improvement for the party, it was far fewer than expected.

The Liberal scaremongering strategy saved the government, but it was wounded. Paul Martin was reduced from a majority to a minority government. That meant the Liberals needed the support of another political party to pass legislation, as parliamentary rules required a majority of votes . It could achieve this majority with support from the Conservatives, which was unlikely, or from the Bloc Québécois, which was equally unlikely.

As fate can decree, the NDP was left one seat short of the twenty seats the Liberals required to form a stable coalition government. Even with the NDP's support, the Liberals could not cast enough votes to carry legislation with a majority. If the NDP had gained this one extra seat, it would have had bargaining power with the government to press for its own policies to be implemented in exchange for NDP support.

* * *

With the election behind us and the summer upon us, a number of the leaders of our missile-defence campaign felt we needed to meet and assess what impact the re-election of the Liberals, albeit with a minority government, would have on our campaign. In our discussion, we returned to our strategy of developing political, communications, and organizing objectives.

As far as political objectives were concerned, we wanted to use Paul Martin's oft-repeated opposition to the weaponization of space to create a bind for him. This would mean making a strong link between space weapons and the missile-defence system.

We had a good working relationship with the NDP, and now we needed to open up lines of communications with each of the other parties, especially the Bloc Québécois. The Bloc Québécois were equally opposed to missile defence, and could have some sway with the Conservatives, since they would like to be "dance partners" in the new minority parliament.

There was a greater opportunity to work with our allies in the Liberal backbenches. We knew there were about thirty Liberal MPs who were opposed to missile defence, but we had no contact with them.

Turning to communications objectives, we realized that we needed to build up the public perception of a link between missile defence and the weaponization of space, which would make it more difficult for Paul Martin to sign on, given his repeated statements in opposition to space weapons.

The media seemed to be consumed by worries about the reaction in the United States to Canada's indecision—or even worse, in their view, the possibility that Canada would actually say "no." We needed to undermine this by demonstrating controversy over the system among Americans themselves, highlighting the fact that there are American as well as Canadian critics.

Finally, looking at organizing objectives, we acknowledged that we had just emerged from a very high state of activities during the election. Now that the summer had arrived, we needed to keep our expectations of what we could ask people to do fairly modest—perhaps letter-writing and more Internet-based lobbying at most.

The next opportunity for action would be when the new parliament began in early October. We had to ensure that missile defence was put at the top of the political agenda. Strategic demonstrations would be a factor in turning up the heat on the prime minister and making the issue a headache for his new minority government.

If we could prevent the Canadian government from joining missile defence over the summer months, then we had an ace in our hand that we could play in the fall. Mel Hurtig, the well-known Canadian publisher and founder of the Council of Canadians, had set his own sights on missile defence and was planning to publish his book on the subject in September. It was entitled *Rushing to Armageddon: The Shocking Truth about Canada, Missile Defence, and Star Wars*.

Every campaign must have messengers, people who are able to deliver the campaign's message through the media to the public in a way that will elicit a positive response. We had been developing a whole roster of experts, celebrities, and politicians to act as our messengers, but Mel Hurtig, because of his influence in Canadian politics, would become one of the most important.

Mel is not a scientist or a diplomat but, because of his work over the years protecting Canadian sovereignty and independence, he has come to be viewed as the nation's nationalist conscience. I was in touch with Mel regularly as he was working on the book and preparing for its launch, which included a fourteen-city book tour across Canada in the fall of 2004, and I knew that he would have a tremendous impact on the public's awareness of what was at stake in Canada's decision to join missile defence.

The more I worked with Mel, the better I came to understand the impact he would have on the debate. His book would provide important information to the public, and his tour would allow him to bypass the media and address thousands of people directly, giving them the information that they were not getting in the daily news.

But even more, because Mel is strongly identified with Canadian nationalism, he could awaken the growing disquiet amongst Canadians about the Bush administration, especially since the U.S. invasion of Iraq. Despite all of the concerns about space weapons and an arms race, I knew that many Canadians would oppose missile defence simply because George W. Bush wanted the system so badly.

If rejection of missile defence became wrapped up in the growing anti-Bush, pro-Canada public sentiment, then any politician who supported missile defence could also be cast as supporting George W. Bush, a man who, according to one poll, was generally viewed by Canadian voters as a greater threat to world peace than Osama bin Laden.

In addition to Mel, we needed a messenger from the United States, preferably someone who could break through this notion that, if we didn't join, the sky would fall on Canada–U.S. relations. Many years ago, I had hosted a public meeting in Vancouver for a remarkable retired U.S. admiral, Rear Admiral Eugene Carroll. Despite the fact that he once had his finger on the nuclear button, after his retirement Admiral Carroll became an outspoken critic of nuclear weapons and founded one of the most important Liberal think-tanks in the United States, the Center for Defense Information. Sadly, he passed away a few years ago, but the tradition of former U.S. military leaders speaking out on important arms-control and disarmament issues—especially those involving nuclear weapons—continues today.

I learned then that the Canadian media held a special reverence for American military men. I chalked it up to a colonial mindset amongst the media. A U.S. military officer was the ultimate expression of U.S. power, which was attractive to many of Canada's elites, including journalists.

In our strategy meeting, we were reminded of a letter that had been sent to President Bush recently that was signed by forty-nine retired U.S. generals and admirals, urging him to scrap the missile-defence system. If we were to have one of these military leaders come to Canada, it would at one and the same time undermine the credibility of the weapon system and show that opposition to missile defence was not anti-American, because there were obviously many Americans who were also opposed to the system.

A member of our group took on the task of contacting our friends in the United States and learning who had organized this initiative. We'd then invite that retired general to come to Ottawa to deliver that message to our own prime minister and the media.

We know now that, in the weeks after the election, Paul Martin had told U.S. ambassador Paul Cellucci that a decision on missile defence was coming. Martin and Defence Minister Bill Graham were preparing to change the NORAD agreement to recognize missile defence. We also didn't know at the time that within a month the campaign was going to take a whole new direction, and we would move from the defensive to the offensive for the first time.

5

ARE WE IN OR OUT?

It was hard to enjoy the summer after the federal election with the missile defence sword of Damocles hanging over our heads. Governments always prefer to make unpopular decisions in the dead of summer while everyone is at the cottage and nobody cares what is happening in Ottawa. That's why we postponed our holidays around the office and kept the campaign going through July and August. We knew a decision to join the missile system could come at any time.

My office phone rang at around 10:30 a.m. on August 5, 2004—an especially hot and sleepy summer day in Ottawa. On the other the end was a reporter from CTV. "Defence Minister Graham's office has called a press conference for 12:30 to make an announcement about NORAD," she said. "We were wondering if you'd be available for a comment afterward." This could be it, the decision we have been expecting, I thought. An announcement to join the missile-defence system may use something concerning the North American Aerospace Defence Command, or NORAD, as a cover. What was the government's game?

We set up a time for me to drop by the CTV studios on Queen Street and hung up. I called Sara and told her the about the reporter's call and Graham's scheduled announcement. "So David Pratt was telling the truth," was Sara's response.

During the election Sara had attended an all-candidates meeting out in the West End of Ottawa, where then-Defence Minister David Pratt was seeking re-election.

During the question period, she had asked Pratt when he thought a decision would be made by the government to join missile defence, and he replied that we would join by the end of the summer.

In the days following the election that left Paul Martin barely clinging to power, I had written a guest column for the *Hill Times*, the weekly newspaper published in Ottawa on all things political, arguing that a decision by the Martin government to join missile defence over the summer would be sheer hubris. "To avoid the mistakes of previous minority governments, Martin needs to govern with some humility. He needs to develop a workable political relationship with Jack Layton and Gilles Duceppe, and he won't want to poison the well with an abrupt missile-defence decision," I wrote.

Well, it wouldn't be the first time I had been wrong. Word of the press conference was travelling fast around Ottawa. A few minutes later I received an e-mail sent to a handful of people from Alexa McDonough's legislative and communications assistant, Anthony Salloum.

Subject: Something's happening today on BMD

Hello Friends, National Defence will announce they have agreed to amend NORAD to include missile detection at 12:30 p.m. today. The release will be on their website at 11:30 a.m.

"'Amend NORAD to include missile detection'? What do you think that means exactly?" I asked Sara. We speculated that the U.S. government had agreed to what the Canadian military had been seeking, which was a central role for NORAD in the U.S. missile-defence system. This would mean that Canadian soldiers assigned to NORAD would be sitting with their fingers on the launch button of the shield's missile interceptors, poised in their silos in Alaska and California.

The defence lobby had been pushing hard for NORAD to play a central role in missile defence. NORAD is treated like a sacred cow in the military—despite the fact that, with the end of the Cold War, the Canada–U.S. alliance that was designed to protect North American skies from Russian bombers and to watch for a surprise Russian nuclear attack no longer seemed as relevant for the defence of North America.

What the Canadian military leadership feared most was any diminishment of the importance of NORAD to their American counterparts. If they lose interest in NORAD, then they lose interest in us, they must have reasoned at National Defence Headquarters on Colonel By Drive in downtown Ottawa.

Canadian generals seem to cherish nothing more that the relationship they have with the U.S. military through NORAD. The U.S. has twenty-four other European allies besides Canada in that other alliance, NATO, but none of them can boast of the special relationship that Canada has with the Americans through our joint NORAD command.

* * *

NORAD was already charged with dispatching U.S. and Canadian fighter planes to shoot down invading Russian bombers, or warning of a Russian or Chinese missile attack. Would the joint Canada–U.S. continental command now be empowered to use missiles to shoot down enemy missiles coming through space to attack North America?

Back in 1958 the United States had decided it needed a continental radar system that could watch the skies for Russian bombers loaded with nuclear bombs coming in over the polar icecap. Back then the nuclear arms race was just getting started, and the only way to lob a big nuke at Washington or Moscow was to drop it from an airplane. Intercontinental ballistic missiles didn't exist yet, so the American plan was to set up radar stations as close to Russia as possible to watch the skies for any possible sneak attacks by Russian bombers.

It takes only a look at a map to figure out why the United States would involve Canada in their plans for fighting a nuclear war—radar stations along the forty-ninth parallel near Buffalo and Seattle just wouldn't be nearly as useful as radar stations in the high Canadian Arctic closer to Russia. Not only would the Air Force have more warning, but the skies over Canada would be the battleground. So Canada was invited to be part of NORAD, the North American Air Defense Command, not so much because the Americans wanted us, but because they needed us.

In the decades that followed, NORAD evolved, and the famous string of radars called the Dew Line was set up in the Canadian Arctic on the West and East coasts to guard the North American approaches. The Commander in Chief of NORAD would always be an American general, but his second-in-command would be a Canadian, our highest-ranking officer in the joint command structure.

The data from the radar stations is sent to NORAD's command bunker complex burrowed deep inside Cheyenne Mountain in Colorado, a facility designed to withstand the explosion of a nuclear bomb. There, Canadians sit alongside Americans watching their computer screens for signs of attack.

Canadian and American fighter planes were permanently assigned to NORAD. During the Cold War they would sit on their runways, sometimes with engines running, waiting for orders to be airborne in fifteen minutes or less. Had NORAD detected an attack, the planes would have been ordered to fly out and attack the intruders with missiles.

The problem of only a handful of planes trying to shoot down waves of incoming bombers was solved by arming those planes' missiles with nuclear bombs of their own. Nuclear weapons would be detonated in the air, destroying dozens of attacking bombers at a time—or so the plan went. Back in the 1960s, even Lester B. Pearson accepted nuclear-tipped Bomarc missiles in Canada as part of the defence of North America.

But like most major weapons system, NORAD's air-defence role was mostly obsolete by the day it was completed. Both Russia and the United States developed intercontinental ballistic missiles armed with nuclear weapons in the late 1950s. This was much more efficient than trying to bomb each other's cities using aircraft. Now a nuclear bomb could be delivered by a missile launched half a world away travelling through the vacuum of space and then re-entering the atmosphere overhead before vaporizing its target in a nuclear inferno.

Therefore, NORAD was given a new mission: to detect missile attacks as well as bomber attacks. New ground-based and space-based technologies were developed to monitor the movement of objects through space and to discern what were pieces of space junk, what were known orbiting satellites, and what were unidentified objects that could be nuclear missiles on their way to attack North America—or anywhere else in the world. NORAD was renamed the North American Aerospace Defense Command to recognize its new role in detecting intercontinental-ballistic-missile attacks.

But the crucial difference between NORAD's original air-defence role and its new aerospace-defence role was that bombers flying through the air could be shot down, but missiles travelling through space and then hurtling back to earth at several times the speed of sound could not. While there was a defence against bombers, there was no defence against missiles.

So this is how we ended up in the bizarre world of the Cold War nuclear strategy called MAD—Mutually Assured Destruction. The theory went that if one side launched a nuclear attack, then the defender would launch its own nuclear attack before the attacker's bombs could reach their targets. The result would be that everyone would die—and so launching a nuclear attack against your enemy would be suicide. Everyone would be destroyed.

NORAD henceforth acted as the United States's early-warning system. Americans and Canadians learned how to detect a missile launch and determine its target. Technically, this was called Integrated Tactical Warning and Attack Assessment (ITWAA), and since Canadians were at the controls some of the time in NORAD, both Canadians and Americans shared in this function.

But while the Americans trusted Canadians to tell them if North America was under attack, Canadians would not be given the authority to actually launch a nuclear counter-strike. This was kept within the power of the U.S.-only Strategic Command, which controlled the nation's nuclear weapons. Only a U.S. president could push the proverbial button.

So an information-sharing arrangement was established that

allowed missile-warning–and-assessment data to be shared with the
U.S.-only Strategic Command. Here one sees the indirect role
Canadians play in the U.S. nuclear-war-fighting strategy. As the ability
to detect missile launches improved to the degree that U.S. satellites
linked into NORAD could detect a launch of even a shorter-range
missile, such as a SCUD, then NORAD's data was shared with U.S.
regional commands such as the CENTCOM, whose area of responsibility is the Middle East.

This was the situation for decades. But the introduction of a system
that could actually shoot down incoming missiles, at least theoretically,
makes things complicated. There was a question mark hanging over
which military command would be given responsibility for launching
the missile-shield interceptors to try to shoot down an attacking missile.
Three possibilities emerged:

The U.S. Strategic Command, which is already responsible for
launching nuclear missiles

The U.S. Northern Command, which is responsible for continental defence, or

The joint U.S.–Canada NORAD, thereby extending its air-
defence role to an aerospace-defence role as well.

The importance the government attached to giving NORAD a "central role" in missile defence indicated that the Canadian military
wanted option number three. Defence Minister David Pratt's letter to
U.S. Secretary of Defense Donald Rumsfeld sought "the closest possible participation." Giving a Canadian the ability to actually launch
missile interceptors was about as close as Canadian military personnel could get.

* * *

In the hour that followed the first notice of Bill Graham's press conference, there was a lot of confusion and speculation about what was
going to be in his announcement. Sara sent out an e-mail to our cross-

Canada list, letting everyone know that an announcement would be coming down in the next few hours. "We are asking that you begin contacting the local media to provide a reaction. Please circulate this message," she wrote.

Ernie Regehr of Project Ploughshares sent back an e-mail reminding us that the Americans had already assigned command of the missile interceptors to the U.S.-only Northern Command, the second scenario mentioned above. Ernie wrote,

Re Something is happening today on BMD

NORAD currently includes detection and tracking of missiles and aircraft, but the defence element includes possible interception of aircraft, but not of missiles. It is not clear that NORAD will be amended to include missile interception, because that role has been formally assigned to NORTHCOM and other U.S.-only commands. But we'll see how this is about to unfold.

It was clear to me that our response time to Defence Minister Graham's announcement would have to be almost instantaneous. The challenge in today's media environment is that there is little time to stand back and study the situation, then prepare your response, and still expect to get some media coverage. In the old days you could craft a thoughtful press release loaded with new facts and pithy quotes from your spokespeople and just send it out to newsrooms hours later. But in today's newsrooms, reporters cover a story and then move on to the next one within hours. To get your view in the news, you must be in the first story written about the topic or event. Forget sitting around writing a press release; to get your view included, you now have to be on the phone with the right reporter while they are writing their story.

This is how the corporate public-relations people do it. Communications specialist Jim Thompson told the *Hill Times* recently that he gave the business lobby high marks for getting its message against a recently proposed reduction to corporate tax cuts out in the media quickly. "What Thomas d'Aquino [of the Canadian Council of Chief Executives] and Catherine Swift [of the Canadian Federation of Independent Business] and the other business lobby groups were doing was making sure that their messaging was injected into the same news cycle as the breaking news," said Thompson. "They wanted to make sure they were in the same news cycle, and that they were the counterpoint to the story of the day, and they were very successful."

According to Thompson, the evolution of the Internet, as well as twenty-four-hour news and other instant media, means that the news cycle is no longer twenty-four hours. "It can be a few minutes. That means that the life of stories is shorter, but it also means that people who are in the media relations business can monitor stories as they develop, and plan how to become a part of those stories," Thompson told the *Hill Times*.

Throughout the missile-defence campaign, we rarely ever had time to write out a press release. Instead, we relied on building personal relationships with reporters, so that we could pick up the phone or send an e-mail to pitch a story and give our take on a new development.

Tracking the daily media coverage of the missile-defence issue and defence policy in general makes you feel as if you know the reporters personally. You get to recognize what kind of story reporters like, who they usually ask for a comment, and whether or not they are willing to go off the beaten path a bit to get a unique and independent perspective, rather than just calling the usual suspects in the defence lobby.

We learned that the best way to get into a story is to develop a one- or two-sentence "line" and call the reporter directly. Leave it on their voice mail if you have to, and if they think it fits in the story, they will call you right back. While not every pitch wins coverage, the contact may put you in their Rolodex and this may result in a call the next time the reporter covers the issue.

* * *

"Okay. What should we be doing right now?" I asked Sara. The fact that a reporter had called us before the press conference had actually occurred was a sign that this was going to be a big story. We decided we needed to be present at Bill Graham's press conference, and to give reporters our line right away. I have seen this kind of "media ambush" approach work in the past when I was at the Council of Canadians. It requires a bit of chutzpa, not to mention skill at getting into the room where the press conference is being held.

I called the CTV reporter back and she told me that Graham's press conference would be held "in the foyer." Sara and I were familiar with the usual press theatres, but I had never heard of this location before. Apparently it was somewhere in the Centre Block, the main building on Parliament Hill where the Peace Tower is located. I called Anthony Salloum in Alexa McDonough's office, "Can you get us to the foyer at 12:30, Anthony?"

The Department of National Defence press release went up on its Web site just after 11:30. Sara printed off a couple of copies and we left the office for the ten-minute walk up to Parliament Hill, reading the release as we went.

News Release
Canada and United States Amend NORAD Agreement
NR 04.058 –August 5, 2004

OTTAWA – Minister of National Defence Bill Graham and Minister of Foreign Affairs Pierre Pettigrew today announced that the Government is amending the North American Aerospace Defence Command (NORAD) agreement with the United States. The amendment authorizes NORAD to make its missile warning function—a role it has been performing for the last 30 years—available to the U.S. commands conducting ballistic missile defence.

The news release went on to emphasize that the amendment maintains the importance of NORAD in continental security and "will preserve the institution's existing missile warning function after the U.S. missile defence system is deployed."

"This isn't what I expected," I said to Sara as we were climbing the steps to the West Block building where Alexa McDonough's office was located. "The good news is that this doesn't appear to be an announcement about joining the missile-defence system, but what does this mean, exactly? Could it be a covert decision to join, camouflaged as some kind of technical agreement?"

Accompanying the press release was the text of letters exchanged between then-Canadian ambassador to the United States, Michael Kergin, and then-U.S. Secretary of State, Colin Powell. The letter from Kergin to Powell demonstrated the kind of contradictory thinking that seemed to be going on inside the Canadian government.

Kergin's letter, dated August 5, 2004 (presumably written by bureaucrats in the department of foreign affairs and approved by the prime minister himself), on one hand reiterated former Defence Minister Pratt's infamous pro-missile-defence letter to Rumsfeld and Rumsfeld's warm reply: "our two Governments should explore extending our partnership to include cooperation in missile defence, as an appropriate response to these new [missile] threats."

But in the next breath, Kergin's letter explicitly signalled that the amendment to the NORAD agreement to allow the "aerospace warning mission for North America also shall include aerospace warning, as defined in NORAD's terms of Reference, in support of the designated commands responsible for missile defence of North America" should not be taken as a decision to join the U.S. missile-defence system. "This decision [to amend NORAD] is independent of any discussion on possible cooperation on missile defence."

Graham's press conference was due to start in a matter of minutes, and we needed to decide quickly what our response was going to be. There was practically no time left to sit and conduct a thoughtful and thorough analysis. The researcher in me wanted to take time and study the announcement in more detail and craft a comprehensive report, but then we would have left the media field to the government. If we didn't get our message out to Canadians, they would have only the government's word to go on.

The announcement brought us to one of the most difficult points in any campaign: defining a "win" and a "loss." In our campaign-planning process, we always ask ourselves, "What does a win look like?" Rarely do events turn out as you expect, and a perfectly clear, unambiguous decision is not what you may end up with. So you need to be clear about your desired goal, so you can hold up developments and see how they compare.

In our missile-defence campaign, our goal was to prevent Canada from joining the U.S. missile-defence program. That seems clear enough, but as the campaign progressed it became increasingly difficult to define the meaning of "join." Join could be a political endorsement of the program, providing funding to the U.S. system or allocating funding for Canadian research or systems which would count as a Canadian contribution to the program, and the use of Canadian territory for radar or missile stations.

If NORAD was to be the command responsible for the system, Canadians could be involved from the planning of the system to actually pushing the button to launch missile interceptors. That was clearly a decision to "join."

There was no question that this was a significant event in the development of the campaign, and we were coming to a fork in the road here. If we decided that sharing data from NORAD with the U.S. command responsible for running missile defence was, in fact, joining missile defence, then our message would have to strongly condemn the government for joining the program and misleading the public by insinuating it hadn't. We would have to tell reporters that, in our view, the government had just joined the program without actually admitting that that is what it had done.

An announcement like this would have signalled to all of the other organizations and our tens of thousands of supporters that the campaign had been lost, "Make a lot of noise, shake your fists and stomp your feet, but at the end of the day pack up your tents and go home."

We arrived at Alexa McDonough's office to meet with her assistant Anthony. Alexa was in her Halifax riding that day. The summer had largely emptied Parliament Hill, with the exception of political staffers, groundskeepers, and tourists. The foyer was next door in the Centre

Block, Anthony told us, as he led us down the hall that linked the West Block to the Centre Block on Parliament Hill. As we followed Anthony through the rabbit warren of parliament's austere stone-walled hallways, we debated what our message should be to the reporters.

Sara was becoming convinced that the NORAD change was the same as a decision to join. "This looks like a decision to join to me. If Canadians are feeding data to the U.S. missile-defence command, then we are part of the system. We should condemn the government for making a deal to join, whether they admit it or not," she said to me.

I felt I didn't have enough information yet, but on a gut level I agreed with Sara. The government was making a clever technical argument to hide the fact that they had given what the defence lobby and the Bush administration wanted: an agreement that NORAD, and hence Canada, would be involved. But if we made that call, it would be the end for the campaign. Game over. It was risky, because the worse thing I could imagine would be telling everyone all was lost when perhaps we were misreading the situation

"We need to get another opinion on this," I said to Sara and Anthony. "Let's find out what Ernie thinks." Ernie Regehr of Project Ploughshares was our team's best resource on the intricacies of the missile-defence issue and the debate within the bureaucracies of foreign affairs and national defence, because of his years of experience in dealing with the government machinery—especially on the issue of NORAD, nuclear weapons, and now ballistic-missile-defence. I left a message at his office asking him to call me back as soon as possible.

The three of us arrived at the foyer, an open space with high, vaulted ceilings and ornate columns just outside the doors that lead into the House's chambers. I immediately recognized it from the evening news as the location where ministers often made announcements to the media at a stand-alone "scrum microphone."

The microphone was set up, with the dark, wooden doors adorned with a Canadian flag as a backdrop. Several TV cameras were set up in front of the mic, and red ropes kept the dozen or more reporters that were waiting for the defence minister's arrival to each side of the microphone to ensure that the cameras had a clear shot of him when he spoke.

After a few minutes Defence Minister Graham and a few of his aides appeared and the press conference began. The camera lights snapped on and the reporters moved in close and held out their tape recorders to capture Graham's comments. Just at that moment my cell phone quietly vibrated in my pocket. "That's Ernie," I said to Sara. "Can you keep an ear on what Graham's saying for me?" Sara moved to the perimeter of the scrum and I retreated to the corner of the room to take Ernie's call.

I told Ernie where we were and that we were going to try to give our own spin to the government's announcement on the NORAD amendment. He had already read the government's press release and the text of Kergin's letter to Colin Powell.

"What do you think Ernie? Is this a covert decision to join missile defence?" I asked him. Ernie replied the he didn't think that this NORAD amendment was the same as a political decision to join. "This new agreement essentially expands the list of consumers of information NORAD has been producing all along, and it's not entirely clear to me why such an amendment was needed ... I think we should hold out for the more important political decision to join missile defence. That way we can live to fight another day," he said. While I was talking to Ernie, I could catch the occasional snippet from Graham, who was speaking to reporters a few feet away: " ... the U.S. intended to create a parallel system ... not a decision to join U.S. system ... preserves NORAD ..."

Out of the corner of my eye, I could see that a plainclothes security guard was becoming interested in me. I guess he was figuring out we weren't reporters here to cover the press conference.

After I finished speaking with Ernie, Sara whispered to me what Graham had been saying. "He says they had to make this decision now, because the Americans were threatening to go and create their own parallel missile warning system to NORAD, and the Canadian government was afraid that this would reduce NORAD's importance to the Americans. He has also said several times that this does not mean Canada has joined missile defence."

Graham was speaking again. "This decision does not affect or in any

way determine the ultimate decision as to whether Canada will participate in missile defence," he said. "That is a decision that remains to be
made by the government and will only be made after extensive consultations with the Cabinet and parliamentarians."

Questions from reporters and Graham's answers were tossed back
and forth.

"What is the timeline for a decision?"

"Not until the fall ... all parties need to be consulted."

"What choice does this leave if Canada wants to opt out?"

"It is not a question of opting out. If we had decided not to do this
today, that would have foreclosed our options. The Americans would
have built a parallel system and there would have been no role for
Canada whatsoever—so this decision preserves our options both ways."

"Is this an incremental step?"

"It doesn't have to be an incremental decision for anything else,"
and with this last comment, Graham abruptly turned away from the
microphone and left the room with his assistant in tow.

"I agree that this looks like a covert way to sign on to missile
defence, but I think we should play it a bit cool until we have time to
do a proper analysis. Let's hold back and say we are concerned and ask
questions, rather than coming out with a hard condemnation—at
least until we get answers to all our questions about the implications
of this NORAD amendment," I whispered to Sara.

The reporters were still taking down their notes and the cameras
were running, so I cleared my throat and said, "Would anyone be interested in an alternate opinion?" I think several of the reporters had
already figured out who we were and why we were there, and so several turned and approached Sara and me. I was starting to introduce
myself when a reporter standing by the camera motioned me to come
over and use the microphone that Graham had been using.

I stepped rather self-consciously to Graham's mic, made a few brief
remarks, and took a number of questions from reporters who kept me
there for quite a while. I spent ten minutes in a media scrum of my
own, practically as long as Graham's. When it was over, I regrouped
with Anthony and Sara. "How'd I do? Did I get it right?"

"Yeah," said Sara. "And you looked very 'ministerial' using Graham's mic."

"I think it's time to go…" said Anthony. It seemed that the plain-clothes security officer was about to move in on us. The three of us got into the elevator.

"Is everything okay?" I asked Anthony.

"Oh, fine. It's just that I didn't know you were going to hold your own press conference using Graham's mic," he said. "That's probably the first time that has ever happened in the history of parliament."

* * *

Our media strategy seemed to work. Many of the news stories that ran that day and the next morning covered our reaction to Graham's press conference. Many of the headlines highlighted our concerns over the defence minister's announcement: "Critics Blast NORAD Update," "Feds Open Door to Role in Missile Defence," "Canada Edges Closer to Star Wars," "Critics Decry Amendment Made to Agreement," "Ottawa Lets U.S. Use Data from NORAD: Missile Defence Plan Closer, Critics; Graham Says Participation Undecided."

In his article, which ran in nine daily newspapers across Canada, the Canadian Press's John Ward wrote, "Critics say the [anti-ballistic-missile] treaty was a cornerstone of international disarmament agreements and that the missile system could start a new arms race, 'What we're seeing is the lack of a political decision being replaced by incremental decisions, small steps, each taking Canada further and further into the missile-defence system,' said Steven Staples, an analyst with the Polaris Institute, an Ottawa-based, non-profit research group."

In the *Toronto Star*, Tonda McCharles wrote, "The left-leaning Polaris Institute, a non-profit research group, said the government's approach is stifling public debate."

Kathleen Harris of the Ottawa *Sun* wrote "U.S. Ambassador Paul Cellucci welcomed the amendment. But Steven Staples, a defence analyst with the Ottawa-based Polaris Institute, raised concerns that there's no assurance from the Bush administration that the pact won't lead to a Star Wars-style weaponization of space."

David Pugliese wrote an article that ran in the *Ottawa Citizen* and the Vancouver *Province*. "'We're trying to appease the Bush administration with this announcement,' said Steve Staples of the Polaris Institute, an Ottawa think-tank opposed to Canadian involvement in the shield."

Alison Myers's story ran as the lead on the CBC radio news, saying, "Steve Staples is with the Polaris Institute, a non-governmental group opposed to missile defence. He says giving NORAD such a vital role in the Americans' proposed system will make it difficult for Canada to back out in the future, 'Each step that we take forward makes it virtually impassible for us to make the political decision that we are not going to join.'"

Even the international news network Reuters reported on our concerns, "Steven Staples of the Polaris Institute think-tank, noting that Thursday's agreement did not mention weaponization of space, said Canada was being gradually drawn into the missile system. 'By the time we're able to have a proper political debate, when parliament resumes in October, in fact there will be very little decision [left] to be made.'"

* * *

Later that afternoon, several of us involved in the campaign held a conference call to share our analysis on the decision and tried to determine the political strategy the government was adopting. Alexa McDonough joined us from her riding in Halifax.

Alexa reported that she had issued a news release and spoken with reporters. She focused attention on Graham's oft-repeated assertion that the future of NORAD would be jeopardized without it being involved in missile defence. "Since 9/11, NORAD has been playing a critical and expanded role in the defence of North America. Bill Graham's suggestion that NORAD's future would be threatened without Canada agreeing to make the 'missile warning function' of NORAD available to the U.S. without any pre-conditions on how the U.S. would use this information is dangerous, misleading, indeed treacherous," said McDonough's release.

Alexa's release pointed out that NORAD's original function in monitoring airspace used by aircraft was much more germane to the security of North America following the obvious danger of hijacked commercial aircraft being used like missiles to attack and kill people, as was the case on the September 11, 2001, terrorist attacks.

NORAD's air-defence role means that it will always play an important role in the defence of North America, which likewise will always require Canadian participation, because of the geography of the continent. Canada actually made a real contribution to this role through radars and other ground- and air-based surveillance equipment and Canadian fighter planes devoted to NORAD for making mid-air interceptions.

In contrast to Canada's contribution to NORAD's air-defence role, the organization's missile-warning and attack-assessment role is almost entirely provided by U.S.-owned-and-operated military satellites. NORAD expert Joseph Jockel, a missile-defence proponent, points out that, in contrast to Canada's significant contribution to NORAD's air-defence role, Canada has little to contribute to aerospace defence (i.e. defence from missile attacks). "The United States would trust the military of no other ally in the assessor position, not even the British. It is striking that the U.S. still feels this way, given how little Canada contributes to North American aerospace defence. There are, in particular, no systems to detect missiles or events in space that are operated by the Canadian military or located in Canada."

Defence Minster Graham asserted that the United States would have had to construct a completely separate, parallel system for missile warning if Canada had not agreed to amend the NORAD agreement to allow the sharing of data with U.S. commands responsible for missile defence. But is this true?

Again, it seems that the government was stretching the truth here. In fact, what is more likely is that NORAD would have been tasked with only an air-defence role for North America, and its missile-warning role and use of the required surveillance equipment would have been handed to another, U.S. command.

As Jockel points out, all the equipment required for missile warning belongs to the United States already. NORAD serves as a collector of information: it receives missile attack warning data from the U.S.

Strategic Command (the command responsible for nuclear weapons), which uses U.S. satellites to monitor missile launches and objects moving through space.

Therefore it is highly unlikely that any new radars, satellites, and the like would have to be paid for and deployed as Graham insinuated in his comment about some parallel system. What is more likely is that data from the U.S. systems transmitted to NORAD would instead be transmitted to a U.S.-only command, most likely NORTHCOM.

All this may seem nicely distinct and separate on paper—but let's remember that, in reality, the personnel for both NORTHCOM and NORAD operate in the same room under Cheyenne Mountain. The U.S.-only NORTHCOM and the Canada–U.S. NORAD share the same U.S. general as their commander (with a Canadian as second-in-command in NORAD).

Had Canada not agreed to the NORAD amendment, the situation could be that the Canadian seated at one computer would monitor aircraft approaching North America, while his NORTHCOM colleague sat next to him watching for aircraft and for missile launches. The distance between Canada being in the system or out of the system would be razor thin anyway.

* * *

In April that year, I had had the chance to test this theory myself directly with a senior U.S. military official from NORAD and NORTH-COM. I had been invited to speak at a conference at Duke University in North Carolina by Michael Byers, who was then a professor of Canadian studies there. He was making considerable waves in the Canadian media on missile defence .

Major-General Raymond F. Rees, Chief of Staff Headquarters, NORAD and U.S. Northern Command, gave a dinner speech on Thursday, April 15, at Duke that outlined the importance of NORAD in protecting North America in the wake of the September 11, 2001, terrorist attacks.

During the question period, I asked him, without revealing my own position, about the validity of concerns expressed in Canada that

NORAD's importance and very future is at risk without Canadian involvement in missile defence.

It was clear from his response that Major-General Rees did not seem to share the missile-defence lobby's concerns. He replied, "We're going to have to be able to make some kind of accommodation if the Canadian government is not going to go along with us on missile defence. We're going to have to come up with some way to proceed so that the United States can conduct missile defence regardless. It is tough and it means we're going to have to change our way. Will that mean the demise of NORAD? I don't believe so. NORAD has a significant role to play with air-breathing threats and with all of the other things I've mentioned here," he said. (The term "air breathing" is a military shorthand term to discern between objects that use air-dependent engines, such as aircraft or cruise missiles, as opposed to objects that can travel through the vacuum of space, such as intercontinental ballistic missiles.)

* * *

On our conference call was the brain trust of our campaign. Our first task was to figure out the technicalities of the government decision. What had actually changed?

"The government spin is around the fact that NORAD is not doing anything new in missile detection. What *is* new will be making the information available to NORTHCOM," said Peggy Mason. Peggy Mason was an advisor to then External Affairs Minister Joe Clark, and later served as Canada's U.N. ambassador for disarmament

"Then perhaps this was less of a technical decision, but more a political decision to send a message to the Americans that Canadians are getting ready to join," I suggested. This, in fact, is precisely how the Americans took the decision. Months later U.S. ambassador Cellucci would tell CTV's Mike Duffy, "Well the approval of the NORAD agreement, I thought was a pretty big signal that this was where the government was heading."

Understanding the technical details of the issue was critical to understanding the government's political strategy. Again, we were coming up against that problem of defining exactly what "joining" missile defence meant. The NORAD amendment did not give Canadians the ability to actually push the button to launch the missile interceptors in Alaska and California to try to shoot down an incoming missile. The arrangement was quite similar to NORAD's decades-long role of watching for Soviet missile attacks, and then passing the information to the U.S.'s Strategic Command, which is responsible for the decision to launch their nuclear weapons in retaliation.

Missile warning and detection in itself, it could be argued, is as useful for preserving peace as it is to waging nuclear war. Transparency is important in building confidence between opposing sides and determining your opponents' intentions.

Think again, for example, of two gladiators standing face to face. Each can see his opponent's stance and judge his intentions. If one gladiator were suddenly blinded by sand in his eyes and could no longer see his opponent, he would most likely lash out wildly with his sword to keep his opponent at bay or perhaps to strike a pre-emptive blow to defend himself.

The critical question is not whether or not to watch for missile launches, but what the government then does with that information. The NORAD missile-warning and tracking information could be used by Northern Command, the U.S. command responsible for operating the missile shield, to target and try to intercept the incoming missile. As Peggy put it, this is the key second phase of missile defence. But in this situation, Canada is not involved in the decision to determine what the response should be, that is, whether to fire the interceptor missiles or not. It is an important distinction.

"Let me add something here about the political implications of this decision," said Douglas Roche, who was also on the conference call. "In my view, what the government has done is essentially create a situation whereby they can delay making a decision on the BMD question. This decision gives the Bush administration what it wants—the use of NORAD's missile warning information for their BMD system."

"So what the government has done is kicked the can down the road until the U.S. election in November," added Doug. "Whoever wins that election will no doubt influence which way the Canadian government goes on BMD."

Doug's analysis was, as it usually is, correct. U.S. Democratic Party presidential candidate John Kerry had come out that week with criticism of President Bush's missile-defence system. "I'm not for rapid deployment of missile defence," Kerry had said in an interview with the U.S. publication *Defense News*. "I don't think we're ready for deployment. I think that's a pool of money that's going to be wasted."

The Canadian government had thrown the Bush administration a bone. The American government could go ahead and declare its system operational in October as it had planned, meeting Bush's campaign promise to deploy a missile-defence system before the end of his term.

"A delay is as good as a win for us," I chimed in. "The longer we can delay a decision to join missile defence, the more time we have to educate Canadians about the dangers that it poses."

In fact, the decision to delay a decision rather than join outright may have been evidence that our campaign was already having an impact. The prime minister's office had received thousands of e-mails opposed to missile defence through Ceasefire.ca. And during the election, missile defence was one of the issues that would always be raised with the prime minister in televised town-hall meetings.

In the days that followed the NORAD amendment, I became confident that we had made the right decision by not declaring this a done deal and continuing to campaign for the much more important political decision to not join missile defence. Even more, the NORAD decision actually created the possibility of a "no" decision on Canadian participation.

Now the Bush administration could not accuse the Canadian government of holding up its ability to go forward. The United States was free to pursue its system as it saw fit, and, since Canadian territory or funding was not needed for them to proceed, the government could separate Canada's decision to join from the ability of the United States to go ahead with its own perceived defensive needs.

Another added bonus was that the NORAD decision essentially clouded what was one of the best arguments for the government to

128 MISSILE DEFENCE

join missile defence: the preservation of NORAD. This had always been a key argument, and then-defence minister John McCallum had listed it as one of the three key objectives in Canada's entering negotiations with the Americans back in May 2003.

This point was brought home to me by an acquaintance from "the other team"—the side promoting Canada joining missile defence. I'll leave him anonymous, but he was active on the conference and media circuit promoting Canada joining (though he was not as ideologically driven as others).

In a private e-mail to me, he wrote,

> What really struck me about the agreement was the cunning of it all. The Liberals secured NORAD and now have true flexibility. If the political winds are against BMD in October, then we decline a larger role. If Canadians miraculously warm to missile defence, we can embrace a larger role. But from my perspective, I no longer see any reason to embrace a larger role. NORAD is secure, the system is imperfect, harms arms control and will lead to weapons in space, and we'll be protected if the system actually works. The air has really been taken out of the pro-BMD argument.

His e-mail suggested to me that even the missile-defence lobby had not seen this government decision coming.

* * *

While we were busy trying to understand the impact of the decision and working through our own reaction to the NORAD amendment, something quite remarkable was happening in the press-conference theatre on Parliament Hill. In fact, the press conference was to set in motion a series of events that would eventually lead to Paul Martin's decision against joining the U.S. missile shield.

Stephen Harper had made the decision not to openly support Paul Martin on missile defence, a position that most observers, including the U.S. ambassador, expected the Conservatives to take. O'Connor was sent to declare that the Conservatives were neither for nor against missile defence, but demanded to see the terms of the deal between Canada and the United States before they would give their endorsement.

At the time nobody had really noticed the significance of this shift. In fact, it took the Conservatives repeating it many times before the Ottawa political and media establishment took notice. Columnists relayed that Conservative support for missile defence meant that Paul Martin would have no problem getting it passed through parliament (even though the government did not require a vote to join; a simple decision by the Cabinet would suffice).

But the Conservatives' attempt to create distance between themselves and the Liberals by insisting on process, rather than agreeing on substance, would eventually be a key factor six months later in Paul Martin's saying "no" to George Bush on missile defence.

A demonstrator on Parliament Hill during U.S. president Bush's visit to Ottawa, November 2004.

The peace group, The Raging Grannies, gives a Valentines Day card to Liberal member of parliament Françoise Boivin for her opposition to missile defence.

Stars Against Star Wars: an open letter to Prime Minister Martin signed by Canadian celebrities including Sarah McLachlan, David Suzuki, Bruce Cockburn, and Steven Page of the Barenaked Ladies. This ad ran in the Toronto Star, the Ottawa Citizen and the Vancouver Sun in the fall of 2004.

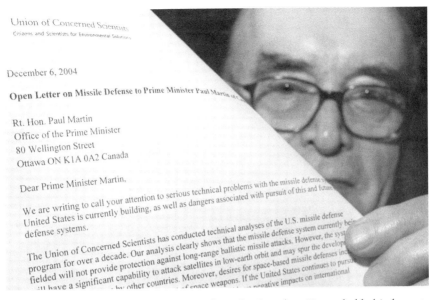

Union of Concerned Scientists
Citizens and Scientists for Environmental Solutions

December 6, 2004

Open Letter on Missile Defense to Prime Minister Paul Martin

Rt. Hon. Paul Martin
Office of the Prime Minister
80 Wellington Street
Ottawa ON K1A 0A2 Canada

Dear Prime Minister Martin,

We are writing to call your attention to serious technical problems with the missile defense
United States is currently building, as well as dangers associated with pursuit of this and futu
defense systems.

The Union of Concerned Scientists has conducted technical analyses of the U.S. missile defense
program for over a decade. Our analysis clearly shows that the missile defense system currently bei
fielded will not provide protection against long-range ballistic missile attacks. However, the sys
:ll have a significant capability to attack satellites in low-earth orbit and may spur the developi
... other countries. Moreover, desires for space-based missile defenses in
... space weapons. If the United States continues to pursu
... negative impacts on international

*Retired U.S. arms control negotiator, Ambassador Jonathan Dean, holds his letter to
Prime Minister Martin warning him about the link between the missile defence
system and space weapons. This photo appeared in the Globe and Mail.*

*Lieutenant General Robert G. Gard, Jr. (US Army, Ret.), the principle organizer of
the anti-missile defence letter sent to U.S. President Bush signed by 49 former generals and admirals, poses before a radar at the Ottawa International Airport for the
Ottawa Citizen.*

Liberal member of Parliament Borys Wrzesnewskyj poses with the Raging Grannies during a demonstration on Parliament Hill.

Mississauga Liberal member of Parliament tells a group of missile defence demonstrators that Canada should not join the "Coalition of the idiots" to great applause.

Members of a "rapid response team" send our anti-missile defence message to Prime Minister Paul Martin and the media in Charlottetown during the 2004 federal election.

Retired U.S. arms control negotiator, Ambassador Jonathan Dean, speaks with Bloc Québécois MP Francine Lalonde following his presentation to the House of Commons Standing Committee on Foreign Affairs and International Trade.

The newspaper headlines announcing the government's decision to not join the U.S. missile defence in February, 2005.

6

TURNING THE TIDE

"Give me your best General face," *Ottawa Citizen* photographer Jana Chytilova ordered the lieutenant general from behind her camera. Lieutenant General Robert Gard, Jr., retired from the U.S. Army, burst out laughing, but followed orders as best he could, pursing his lips and lowering his eyebrows. She snapped the photo.

The three of us were standing in the middle of a little-used road a few dozen metres from the main runway at the Ottawa International Airport, shouting at each other to be heard over the roar of jet-airplane engines. It was a great location for a photograph of General Gard because in the background was a six-storey-high radar dome.

The next morning, August 10, 2004, copies of the *Ottawa Citizen* landed on doorsteps across the city. Inside was an article bearing the headline "Missile Shield Won't Protect Canada: Expert." Below it was Jana's photo of General Gard standing in front of the ominous radar dome, arms crossed, staring directly into the camera's lens. Looking closely at the photo, I could see the faint flicker of a repressed smile behind his put-on official expression. The article itself was written by defence reporter David Pugliese. Pugliese had interviewed General Gard just before he boarded his plane at Reagan National Airport in Washington, D.C., for the flight to Ottawa, where the photographer and I were waiting to greet him.

"The United States' missile shield will offer little protection to

Canadians and most likely will never work, says a U.S. general who is one of several dozen retired senior military officers opposing the untested system," said the article. It continued:

> Retired Lt.-Gen. Robert Gard, Jr., says one of the biggest threats facing the U.S. is not a ballistic missile fired by Iran or North Korea, but that of terrorists or "rogue nations" smuggling a weapon of mass destruction into the country and detonating it. "We're spending money on a [anti-missile] system that most probably will not work against an unlikely threat while we're under-funding programs designed to counter the more likely threat," [said Gard.]

The article was the beginning of a whirlwind two days in Canada for General Gard. He appeared on talk shows, was interviewed by the press, met with politicians and the Ottawa defence and foreign-policy community. He was here at the invitation of my organization, the Polaris Institute, and our partner group, Physicians for Global Survival. A small grant from the Toronto-based Walter and Duncan Gordon Foundation made General Gard's trip possible.

For me, the extremely high level of media interest in General Gard was not surprising at all. My past experience had shown that U.S. military personnel were always in high demand by the Canadian media—especially when their message ran counter to the policies of the U.S. government and the Canadian government.

General Gard's credentials are extensive. He is a veteran of both the Korean and the Vietnam wars, and served many years—from the late 1970s until he retired in the late 1980s—as president of the National Defense University. His career then took an interesting turn when he spent more than a decade as the president of the Monterey Institute of International Studies. The institute is also the home of the progressive Monterey Center for Non-Proliferation.

After leaving the institute, General Gard became a consultant to several arms-control organizations, including the Vietnam Veterans of America Foundation. The veterans' group helped found the campaign to forge an international ban on anti-personnel land mines and went on to win the Nobel Peace Prize. "One of my proudest moments was attending the Ottawa signing ceremony for the land-mines treaty," General Gard told me on the drive in from the airport.

He was in Ottawa as an adviser to the Washington, D.C.–based Center for Arms Control and Non-Proliferation. He had become an outspoken critic of missile defence in the United States, and in early 2004 he had organized an open letter to President Bush on missile defence that was signed by forty-nine retired generals and admirals.

The letter to President Bush criticized the missile shield as being an untested and expensive system that would not defend anyone from a nuclear missile attack:

> The Pentagon has waived the operational testing requirements that are essential to determining whether or not this highly complex system of systems is effective and suitable…. Another important consideration is balancing the high costs of missile defense with funding allocated to other national security programs.

> As you have said, Mr. President, our highest priority is to prevent terrorists from acquiring and employing weapons of mass destruction. We agree. We therefore recommend, as the militarily responsible course of action, that you postpone operational deployment of the expensive and untested GMD [Ground-based Midcourse Defense] system and transfer the associated funding to accelerated programs to secure the multitude of facilities containing nuclear weapons and materials and to protect our ports and borders against terrorists who may attempt to smuggle weapons of mass destruction into the United States.

The letter echoed many of the concerns of former Clinton-administration "terrorism czar" Richard A. Clarke, who had argued for the same focus. But as Clarke pointed out in his book *Against All*

Enemies, the Bush administration was fixated on only two priorities: invading Iraq and building a missile-defence system.

From our standpoint in Canada, neither the high cost of missile defence nor its functionality was our chief concern. Our arguments against missile defence focused mainly on the risk of provoking another nuclear-arms race and the weaponization of space, in addition to the broader abandonment of Canada's traditional support for arms control and peacekeeping. While General Gard's letter did not specifically address these points, his message was going to move us in the same direction—away from joining an unworkable system.

I felt that he would be our most important messenger for the campaign, and our goal was to have him heard by as many Canadians as possible. We had been planning his visit for several weeks, and we were so worried that the government would make a snap decision to join missile defence in the middle of the summer that we scheduled him to come to Ottawa in the dead of August, rather than wait for the fall, a typically more appropriate time to bring in a guest speaker.

But as it turned out, the timing was perfect. The government had just made its announcement about allowing NORAD to share missile-launch warning information with the U.S. Northern Command, which was charged with running the continental shield.

Besides, despite our initial grave concern about the NORAD decision, I was coming to believe that the previous week's announcement was going to help us in three important ways. The first was that it put the issue back in the media spotlight again. Second, it seemed to remove the government's strongest argument, which was that not joining missile defence would jeopardize the future of NORAD. The third, and most important, was that it seemed to indicate that Paul Martin had delayed, once again, making a decision on missile defence.

The wind was shifting on missile defence, and for the first time we were moving from the defensive to the offensive. I found concrete evidence of this in the subtle alteration that was occurring in the coverage of missile defence that summer. For instance, after meeting General Gard, *Globe and Mail* columnist Hugh Winsor wrote:

Why did [former defence minister] Mr. Pratt go begging in January, beseeching the Pentagon to amend the NORAD agreement in the first place? (This move was initiated by Canada, not, as is conventionally believed, a response to a request from Washington.)

As Gen. Gard puts it, [the missile shield] amounts to putting "a useless scarecrow in the sky, that is unlikely to ever work as envisioned" ... and therein lies a tale. There is not one Canadian general or civilian military planner at National Defence Headquarters who believes the NMD [National Missile Defence] is likely to work. But there is an overwhelming concern to maintain the relevance of NORAD, the only binational organization where a Canadian gets to sit next to the big boys, almost as equals... .

Fortunately the modifications to the NORAD agreement announced this month don't amount to much... . As General Gard and his co-panelist Peggy Mason (a former Canadian disarmament ambassador) put it, NORAD is more, not less, relevant after the terrorist attacks of Sept. 11, 2001... .

The current chief of staff at NORAD, General Raymond Rees, agrees. He told a recent seminar at Duke University, NMD or no NMD, NORAD would continue to be a core element of North American defence.

By the end of General Gard's two days in Ottawa, he had conducted a press conference that had been carried live on national television, spoken to a sold-out Newsmakers Luncheon at the National Press Club, been interviewed on morning TV shows on CTV and CBC, and had done live radio interviews on two national CBC Radio programs, *The Current* and *The House*, as well as scores of other interviews with private broadcasters and newspapers. The poor man had a cellphone to his ear almost every available minute.

The result was more than fifty newspaper stories about the U.S. general who was opposed to missile defence. Many of the stories were accompanied by a photo of him, dramatically increasing the article's prominence. The headlines were powerful: "Missile Shield a Waste, Ex-General Says"; "Missile Shield Useless to Canada: General"; "Defence Plan under Attack"; "Axe Missile Shield: Retired U.S. General"; "Missile Defence Is Costly and Unproven, Critics Say"; "Ex-U.S. General Slams Missile Defence System"; "Missile Cash Could Be Better Spent: General"; "Le Canada doit rejeter le bouclier antimissiles"; "Missile Defence to Test Martin's Rule"; "Un général américain à la retraite s'oppose au bouclier antimissile"; "Le Canada doit se retirer du projet de bouclier antimissile, dit un ex-général américain"; "Martin Faces Incoming Barbs Over Missile Defence"; and so on.

In addition to the media interviews, we met with MPs from three political parties, the Conservatives, the Liberals, and the NDP. The second day, August 11, General Gard, former UN ambassador for disarmament Peggy Mason, and I boarded a plane for Toronto. Our destination was a small office complex in Mississauga, the location of Liberal MP Carolyn Parrish's constituency office.

When we arrived we were greeted by Carolyn and General Gard was introduced to four other area Liberal MPs: Bonnie Brown from Oakville, Lynn Myers from London, and Navdeep Bains and Wajid Khan from Mississauga. General Gard took his place at the end of the table next to Carolyn and gave a briefing for the MPs that laid out a damning critique of Bush's system.

He told them how, in the Bush administration's rush to deploy the system by that fall of 2004, many of the essential components of the missile-defence system had been assembled without proper testing of each one. This meant that it would be very difficult, if not impossible, to identify the source of malfunctions without taking the whole system apart. Gard was later proven right, when untested interceptor missiles didn't launch during tests.

Further, an enemy merely had to ensure that its missile could camouflage its warhead with decoys as it travelled through space, in order to make it impossible for the missile shield's "kill vehicle" to collide with the nuclear warhead instead of a dummy. This problem of missile discrimination was being utterly overlooked by the weapons designers because it was an unsolvable problem.

The Liberal MPs hardly needed convincing. Carolyn Parrish had already made her own opposition to the system known, and she and Bonnie Brown and Lynn Myers were leaders among members of the Liberal caucus opposed to the system. "Just give me the information," Carolyn Parrish said. "I'm a great lobbyist."

The MPs said they had been receiving calls from Defence Minister Bill Graham, Martin's senior advisers, and even Paul Martin himself to convince them to drop their opposition. Parrish told us, "Paul called me and said, 'But Carolyn, aren't you concerned about the safety of North America?' I said, 'Yes I am; that's why I am opposed to this system.'"

Carolyn Parrish was careful not to criticize Martin directly, but felt that he was surrounded by advisers who were misinforming him. However, she pointed out to us, Martin could be moved. "Keep up the pressure," she told us.

* * *

Our August meeting with the Liberal members of parliament was an important breakthrough in the campaign. It opened up a new "front" for us, and our objective was to bring as many Liberal backbench MPs over to our view as possible. Paul Martin was now navigating his way through a minority parliament, in which he needed every vote in order to keep his government in power. Liberal backbenchers had power and influence in this new minority parliament; they could not be taken for granted by Paul Martin.

Ironically, it was Paul Martin himself who tilled the soil that would allow opposition to missile defence to take root in the party. During his leadership campaign he championed open discussions about policies and promised to address what he called "the democratic deficit" in Canadian politics. It was a pledge that appealed to the Liberal ranks that had been largely left out of Liberal Party power circles during the Chrétien years. The result was that expectations were raised, and

Liberal MPs now wanted to be consulted on policy matters and be permitted to express their views openly.

Paul Martin raised the expectations of Canadian voters as well. He stoked nationalist sentiments by inviting rock star Bono to come to the Liberal convention and declare, "The world needs more Canada."

No doubt the day after the election Martin probably regretted having said many of the things he had in the preceding year. According to many who know him well, Paul Martin is not a pink Liberal at all, but a corporate-backed fiscal conservative who wanted closer ties to the United States, not more distant ones. It's a pretty good bet that, had Paul Martin been prime minister in 2003, Canadian troops would be fighting and dying in Iraq alongside U.S. troops.

In fact, those closest to him have said that Paul Martin is very controlling and has difficulty delegating. From the moment he became prime minister, he insisted on being involved in all major decisions. This fact, combined with his own penchant for exhaustively debating the issues with advisers, meant that his office became a bottleneck, and many policies languished while waiting for a decision from the top. Empowering backbenchers, especially any MPs who were closely aligned to his predecessor, Jean Chrétien, was the last thing he wanted to do. The way he ruthlessly cut former Chrétienites from Cabinet and other positions of influence bears this out.

With the election behind them, Liberals were now looking ahead to the new parliament and to learning how to govern without a majority. It was our strategy to ensure that missile defence became such a headache for Martin that he would be forced to go against his inclination to join the U.S. system, if only to preserve unity in his party and therefore his hold on 24 Sussex Drive.

On August 11, 2004, an *Ottawa Citizen* headline showed that the ball was in motion already: "Martin Travels 'Tightrope' on Missile Defence." Reporter Kate Jaimet had spoken to Carolyn Parrish and Lynn Myers about missile defence and about how the issue would affect the new Martin minority government. Parrish said that Martin needed to strike a balance between appeasing the United States and listening to a "large chunk" of his caucus that opposed missile defence: "In this case he may be able to get the Tories [to support the missile shield] ... but what you would be doing is damaging your chance to keep the NDP on side for future issues that would be more socially based," said Parrish.

"This is a man who came to power saying he wanted to address the democratic deficit," added Parrish. "If those who are against [missile defence] can convince those who are in the middle, and we end up with 50 percent plus one against it, I think he's going to have to look at that long and hard, because he's made a commitment to re-democratize the system."

Lynn Myers pointed out that, despite the fact that the government could join missile defence without a vote in parliament, MPs would still be required to vote on the federal budget, which could contain funding to pay for Canada's contribution to missile defence. "If it was an appropriations bill, that ... is a matter of confidence, which makes the whole decision-making process even murkier," said Myers. If a minority government loses on a budget vote, it is considered a vote of non-confidence and the government is forced to call an election immediately.

General Gard's visit wasn't needed to convince these Liberals of the folly of missile defence, but his high-profile comments and his respected background provided backbenchers with greater legitimacy for their views. Missile-defence critics could now quote a retired U.S. general who shared their skepticism about missile defence, as Parrish did for the *Hill Times*: "[General Gard] thinks it's jeopardizing us rather than making us safer."

* * *

Parliament was set to reconvene in the first week of October 2004. The prime minister's office was setting out a timetable of events to place the government in the best possible position for the new session. The prime minister announced his new Cabinet and met with the premiers in August to promise new funding for health care. In late August, he would meet with the Opposition party leaders, hold a retreat for his caucus in Ottawa, and preside over the first meeting of his new Cabinet.

We searched for every opportunity that we could use to increase the pressure on Martin before parliament reconvened in October. The NDP and the Bloc Québécois remained opposed to missile defence, so we concentrated on building resistance within the Liberal caucus itself.

Two weeks after General Gard's visit to Canada, every Liberal member of parliament was going to come to Ottawa to plan for the coming session of parliament. The three-day retreat, from August 23 to 25, would include meetings of the various party committees, leading to a meeting with the prime minister in what party officials described as "dialogue" between the prime minister and the MPs. "[Missile defence] will be brought up," Carolyn Parrish told the *Hill Times*.

Sara put together a briefing binder of the latest information and critiques of the missile-defence system for Parrish, and copies were also sent to the NDP's Alexa McDonough and the Bloc Québécois's foreign-affairs critic Francine Lalonde. We kept in touch with the offices of Parrish, Myers, and Brown as the Liberal retreat drew closer.

On Monday, August 23, the first day of the Liberal meeting in Ottawa, Martin had two loud shots fired across his bow. He knew then that missile defence was already shaping up as a serious threat to his fragile minority government.

The first shot occurred that morning. Martin met with the Opposition leaders individually, hoping to build a consensus on a way to make the new government work. Conservative leader Stephen Harper was tight-lipped about his meeting, but not the NDP's Jack Layton.

The NDP was set to make missile defence a key issue in the coming session. "It is a fundamental issue for us," Layton told reporters after his meeting with Martin, adding that the Liberals could expect no compromise from the NDP on the matter. "We do not believe Canada should be part of the weaponization of space."

The second shot came later that day. Missile defence quickly had risen to become the top issue—especially for women MPs. Many members who attended the women's caucus committee meeting expressed grave concerns about joining Bush's plan. The women's caucus was already upset that Martin had appointed so few women to Cabinet, and now the women MPs were coming together around the missile-defence issue.

Sarmite Bulte, a top Ontario MP and head of the federal Liberals' Ontario caucus, told a Canadian Press reporter that the federal government should immediately turn its back on the missile-defence project and that Liberal women should help lobby to make it happen. "Do I believe that's something that women should unite about? Yes," Bulte said.

The next day, Sara and I met in my office to pore over the missile-defence coverage. It was a Tuesday morning. "Paul Martin is meeting with the entire caucus tomorrow afternoon inside the parliament buildings. We need to keep up the momentum, and make sure that missile defence is front and centre," said Sara.

"Okay, let's see if we can get hundreds of people to send e-mails in to Liberal MPs who are speaking out against missile defence. We want them to feel they have public backing in their challenging of Martin's gang in the prime minister's office," I said. "And do you think we could get Carolyn Parrish, Lynn Myers, and Bonnie Brown to address a rally in front of the Peace Tower just before Martin meets with the caucus?"

"I can call their offices and find out," said Sara.

We had our answer within an hour: Parrish, Brown, and Myers were willing to speak to a group of demonstrators on the front steps of the Parliament Buildings the next day at noon hour. The demonstration would be timed for the final day of the Liberal caucus meeting and would occur moments before all the MPs gathered for a closed-door meeting with Prime Minister Martin. Carolyn had already said she was going to raise the issue in the meeting, but news cameras and reporters wouldn't be allowed inside. The rally would give her moral support, and provide some footage for the evening news as well.

Sara contacted our local activists in Ottawa, urging them to join us on Parliament Hill the next day for the missile-defence demonstration. The Raging Grannies agreed to come and sing a few of their satirical protest songs. Others started putting together anti-missile-defence banners and placards. We also heard from activists in Toronto, who planned to hold a demonstration outside Defence Minister Bill Graham's riding office.

In addition to our organizing in Ottawa, working with our Web experts we set up a special Web page on Ceasefire.ca that allowed people to send this message to the Liberal MPs who were speaking out against missile defence: "I support your opposition to Canada joining the U.S. missile defence system, and encourage your every effort to work within the government and the Liberal Party to prevent Canada from joining this expensive and dangerous system."

I quickly wrote up a letter to the roughly fifteen thousand people who had become part of the campaign through our Ceasefire.ca Web site. I encouraged them to visit the Web site and send their letters of support to the Liberal backbenchers. The letters from campaign supporters soon started flooding into the MPs' offices.

The last step was to notify the media. That afternoon we sent out a media release to all the newsrooms in Ottawa:

Media Advisory – Gatherings to Show Support for Liberal Members of Parliament Who Are Opposed to Missile Defence

OTTAWA, Aug. 24, 2004: Activists will gather on Parliament Hill in Ottawa tomorrow, and at Defence Minister Bill Graham's office in Toronto, to show support for Liberal MPs Carolyn Parrish, Bonnie Brown, Lynn Myers and others who are opposed to the U.S. missile-defence program. Canada's role in the controversial missile-defence system will be discussed at the Liberal Caucus meetings on Wednesday, August 25, 2004.

"Carolyn Parrish, Bonnie Brown and Lynn Myers have shown great leadership on the missile-defence issue, and their vocal opposition resonates with many Canadians," said Sara Kemp, Coordinator of the Canadian Campaign to Oppose Missile Defence.

12:45 p.m., Wednesday August 25, 2004, Parliament Hill MPs Carolyn Parrish (Mississauga–Erindale) and Bonnie Brown

(Oakville) will greet the gathering at 12:45 p.m.

The Raging Grannies will also be on hand to sing a few satirical songs on missile defence.

Organized by the Canadian Campaign to Oppose Missile
Defence

Late Wednesday morning, Sara and I gathered up every available
staff person in our office, and the half-dozen of us made our way from
our office up to Parliament Hill. We'd had less than twenty-four hours
to put our plan in place, but everything seemed to be coming together.
By that morning, nearly a thousand people had used the Ceasefire.ca
Web site to send e-mailed letters of support to Liberal backbenchers
opposed to missile defence.

Our group joined about thirty people on Parliament Hill. The purpose of the rally was not to show broad-based public opposition to
missile defence, but to create a respectable-sized audience for our MPs
to address. We had enough people for our media event, and about a
dozen cameras and reporters were hovering around waiting for the
action to start.

Someone had brought a banner, and we unfurled it on the steps. It
said, "BMD: Misguided men make guided missiles." The wording was
appropriate, considering that leadership against missile defence was
coming from many women. The Raging Grannies were already there,
along with Gerry Barr from the Canadian Council for International Co-
operation, Debbie Grisdale, Mel Watkins, some colleagues from other
groups such as the Council of Canadians and other peace groups, and
even some students.

Sara stood on the steps in front of the banner and began addressing
the crowd. She made a few comments and asked the Raging Grannies
to sing a song. But there was no sign of our MPs. Sara pulled Gerry Barr
from the crowd and asked him to make a few remarks, then I spotted
Lynn Myers speaking with reporters nearby.

Carolyn Parrish finally arrived. Sara thanked Gerry, and introduced

Carolyn. The crowd applauded, the media moved in closer, and Carolyn began her remarks.

First she said that her office had received more than nine hundred letters of support for her, and only one e-mail in favour of missile defence. Then, with a half-smile, she said, "I have some good news for you. We are not joining the coalition of the idiots; we are joining the coalition of the wise." There was applause and cheers, and then she went on to explain why she and so many others were opposed to missile defence, and said they were going to urge Paul Martin not to join the U.S. system.

"There's the quote," Guy Caron from the Council of Canadians said in my ear.

"What's that?" I said. We were standing in the small crowd listening to Carolyn.

"That's the line that will be on the news. 'Coalition of the idiots,'" he said.

I have to admit the comment had gone right by me. How else would one describe a system that cost ten billion dollars a year, had no chance of working, and was intended to defend us from a non-existent missile threat? Idiotic did not seem an inappropriate description to me.

When Carolyn finished, she turned and started to walk back towards the Parliament Buildings, but I asked her if she wanted to hold a "scrum" with the reporters. We approached a group of reporters, and they interviewed her for a few minutes. I was called away and didn't hear the interviews, but it was at this point that reporters asked her if she was calling George W. Bush an idiot. She said no, that it was the plan that was idiotic, and then rather unfortunately asked them not to report on the comment.

Carolyn's "coalition of the idiots" remark went off like a bomb. When we got back to the Polaris Institute's office we saw that the media were jumping all over it. Of course, since Carolyn only a year earlier had said, "Damn Americans. I hate those bastards," the reporters were waiting for any less-than-gentle remark to seize upon. And Carolyn had given it to them.

Naturally, the reporters went to the prime minister to get his reaction—especially to ask him if he intended to discipline Parrish. "You are going to get strongly held views" on the missile-defence debate, he told reporters that afternoon. "But let me tell you, those [views] need to be expressed in language that's acceptable."

Conservative Party defence critic Gordon O'Connor said that Martin should kick Parrish out of the Liberal caucus. "There is no need to put the stick in the eye of the U.S. government by these comments," he told CTV News. For his part, U.S. ambassador Paul Cellucci was uncharacteristically nonchalant about the comment, telling the CBC, "Canada is a free country; people can express their opinions how they see fit."

Carolyn's comment had many different effects. It firmly placed missile defence within the realm of Canada–U.S. relations, especially our relationship with President George W. Bush. So there was a lot of "weeping and gnashing of teeth" by those members of the elite who were seeking closer ties to the United States.

CBC-TV news anchor Peter Mansbridge could barely disguise his disdain. That night he opened his newscast by implying that Parrish had insulted our greatest trading partner:

> Good evening. Today's meeting of the Liberal caucus in Ottawa was supposed to be many things. A brainstorming session, a chance to air grievances in public and to prepare for the Throne speech in October. It wasn't supposed to include public insults or cramp Canada's relations with its largest trading partner. And it certainly wasn't supposed to make the Prime Minister look bad. But it may have done all those things.

Give me a break. She didn't mention George W. Bush, or even the United States, for that matter. Parrish was simply expressing a view that many Canadians held, and it was clearly done in jest. In fact, one admittedly unscientific poll on the CTV Web site showed that a majority of respondents, 56 percent, said that Canada should not lend its political backing to the U.S. missile-defence plan.

Ottawa Citizen columnist Susan Riley used her razor-sharp writing to skewer her colleagues in the media, calling them "a coalition of the prudish." She wrote, "In their anxiety not to give offence (for fear of trade or diplomatic reprisals), the Bush apologists in our media and the opposition parties are more Catholic than the Pope—and far more deferential than most ordinary Americans. This tendency to self-censorship is what is embarrassing for a grown-up country, not the odd colourful insult."

CBC-TV's coverage also showed that many of Parrish's colleagues shared Carolyn's concern. Bonnie Brown said, "I don't want Canadians and ... the Canadian government to be part of something that, in my view, even American generals think is not going to work." Former Cabinet minister Maria Minna said, "My concern is that it increases proliferation of arms instead of preventing it."

Nevertheless, I was concerned that, by playing into her opponents' hands, by giving them the ammunition to pillory her with, Carolyn had stigmatized herself in the debate, and possibly had driven other potential missile-defence opponents in the party scrambling for cover.

A quick media snapshot of most newspapers in Canada shows that missile defence dominated the headlines that week. There were more than 230 news reports, editorials, commentaries, letters to the editor, and other articles about missile defence during the week. But in the days that followed, it was difficult to gauge the political impact of Carolyn's comments. Would there be a backlash against missile-defence critics, branding them as impolite anti-Americans who risked hurting the U.S.-trade-dependent Canadian economy, as Peter Mansbridge had suggested?

My assessment was this: while Carolyn may have damaged her own future role in the debate, overall she helped us to achieve our objectives of putting missile defence at the top of the political agenda, and she demonstrated to Paul Martin that this issue would continue to dog him and his party. Missile defence would be a liability for him, and the easier decision would be to not join the program.

Already, the controversial issue had spoiled what Martin had intended to be a smooth transition from the election to the formation of a government. The day after Parrish's comments, reporters asked Cabinet minister Judy Sgro, as she walked into Martin's first Cabinet meeting, what she thought of Parrish. An obviously angry Sgro shot back, "She should have kept her mouth shut!" Clearly, all was not well in the House of Liberals.

* * *

A postscript on Carolyn Parrish's impact on the missile-defence debate:

On November 18, 2004, about three months after that August demonstration on Parliament Hill, we organized a visit to Ottawa by Alan Simpson, a member of Tony Blair's government and an ardent critic of nuclear weapons and missile defence. We asked Alan to tell Liberal MPs about his experience as a backbencher of a governing party that had joined the U.S. missile-defence system, sharing his experience of the secret deals and lack of information that were commonplace in the British debate on missile defence. Our schedule included a press conference and meetings with MPs, including a meeting in the afternoon with Carolyn Parrish and Lynn Myers. The times and locations of all of our meetings were included in our press release, which was distributed widely.

At the appointed time, Alan, Sara, Peggy Mason, and I were navigating our way through the maze of corridors in the Centre Block to get to the room where we were to meet with Parrish and the others. As we got closer we turned down a hallway and were startled to come face to face with a crowd of reporters and cameras so large that it blocked the entire hallway. Some camera lights snapped on, and we were so surprised that we dodged them and went down another hallway. "What was that all about?" I said to Sara as she checked the directions to the meeting place.

"Those reporters are standing outside our meeting room," she said, checking the map.

The penny dropped. The reporters weren't waiting for us; they were waiting for Carolyn to arrive at our meeting. Carolyn was back in the news because the night before she had appeared on a comedy program in which she was stomping on a little voodoo doll of George W. Bush. It was obviously a very funny bit of self-parody, but of course the "Coalition of the Prudish" media didn't see it that way, nor did Prime

Minister Martin. Unbeknownst to us, he had just expelled Carolyn from the Liberal caucus, forcing her to sit as an independent.

We gathered ourselves together and went back down the hall to our meeting, squeezing our way through the phalanx of reporters. It was very awkward, and no one said a word. With the reporters outside the door, Lynn informed us of Carolyn's fate. We went ahead with our meeting, and Alan spoke to Lynn and an MP whom I had never met before, Borys Wrzesnewskyj from Etobicoke Centre. He was a colleague of Lynn's.

During a break, Lynn and Borys had a brief conversation that I thought was very revealing, and I hoped indicative of what was happening inside the Liberal Party. Lynn asked Borys how he thought he would vote in the anticipated, non-binding vote on missile defence. Borys replied, "At first I accepted the reasons they [Liberal Party officials] were giving for why we should the missile-defence system, but I still had a few questions. So I asked them for a little more information, but I never got a reply. I read and heard a bit more about missile defence, and so I asked my questions again—and still did not get a reply. Now, I just don't know how I am going to vote."

By February 2005, Borys had decided. Only a few days before Martin would announce that Canada would not join missile defence, Borys joined Jack Layton and Science for Peace's John Valleau at a community meeting on missile defence in Toronto. At the meeting, Borys said he would not vote for missile defence. "The U.K. signed on and it cost then a billion dollars in research," he said, most certainly as a result of his meeting with our guest from the United Kingdom.

"[Prime Minister Lester] Pearson had a vision that young Canadian men and women should not travel to trouble spots as soldiers, but as peacekeepers," the *Etobicoke Guardian* quoted him as saying. "In the twenty-first century, Canada should expand on that: peacekeeping and civil society building."

7

THE QUEBEC FACTOR

I've never met Jack Granatstein in person, but I always imagine him to be a bit like that 1970s TV character Archie Bunker. Conservative and always harkening back to "the good old days." Archie was always butting heads with his hippie son-in-law in the weekly series *All in the Family*.

True, Jack Granatstein is a highly regarded and accomplished Canadian military historian, who has written books with titles like *Who Killed the Canadian Military?* (in which he blames pretty well everyone). He even runs his own military lobby group, which he called the Council for Canadian Security in the 21st Century. In fact, among military buffs, he is regarded as their sage.

But Jack Granatstein is a military man's man, nostalgic for the Cold War—or even better, the Second World War. Now that was a simpler, better time, when everyone knew who was the good guy and who was the bad guy by the colour of his uniform. Forget modern talk of soft power and touchy-feely UN peacekeeping. Granatstein yearns for the days when wars were fought for God and country.

Jack Granatstein, not surprisingly, was strongly in favour of Canada joining the Iraq war and missile defence. Nearly three years after Canada declined to join the war and a year after the missile-defence decision, he was still complaining publicly about the government's decisions to stay out of both.

In an article he wrote for the *Vancouver Sun* newspaper, published on January 2, 2006, Granatstein said, "I was in favour of supporting the U.S. in Iraq and joining the missile-defence project. My reasons were based on our national interests. Canada's economy depends on trade with the U.S. and that cannot be changed. We are extremely vulnerable if the U.S. is unhappy with us." To his credit, he was honest in admitting that his main motivation for joining missile defence and the invasion of Iraq had nothing to do with the defence of Canada or our own independent assessment of international security needs. It was all simple financial self-interest for Canada: what George W. Bush wants, George W. Bush should get.

The fact that Canada said "no" on both counts and suffered no demonstrable economic impacts whatsoever is conveniently overlooked by Granatstein, as well as the editors of the *Vancouver Sun* who agreed to print the article.

Granatstein tried to lay the blame for the decisions on Quebec:

> I would suggest that the decision to refuse to join in the U.S. ballistic-missile shield program in 2005 again was shaped by overwhelmingly hostile Quebec poll numbers—and by the Liberals' minority-government situation.... It is bad for unity to have Quebec setting the agenda on Iraq or missile defence. On both Iraq and missile defence, the poll numbers were supportive in English Canada; on Iraq, there was at one point a 40-per-cent-plus difference between Alberta and Quebec on support for the war.

Granatstein concluded by accusing Martin of pandering to Quebec and minorities: "Trying to give Quebec what it wants hurts the country ... I know that multiculturalism is a core value of the Liberal Party—and the Conservative Party and the NDP. But Prime Ministers must lead nationally, and aspiring prime ministers must do this too. Look after the nation's interests first and values second."

This "blame Quebec" analysis—the belief that missile defence was lost because of polling numbers in Quebec—is promoted by backers of missile defence and the Iraq war. I heard a similar comment from former Major General Lewis MacKenzie when I debated him on television in late 2005. During the debate he argued that, if you took Quebec out of the calculation, a majority of "Canadians" supported joining the invasion.

Personally, I find this argument has a bit of a nasty, anti-Quebec odour. It's no surprise that much of the pro-military commentary emanates from Alberta, the birthplace of the Reform Party, which is often associated with anti-Quebec sentiment.

The University of Calgary serves as home to several right-wing defence experts as well as the defence-industry-backed Canadian Defence and Foreign Affairs Institute, the latest defence lobby group to appear on the scene.

But is this argument backed by the facts? Was missile defence defeated merely because the prime minister was afraid of polling numbers in Quebec? And what exactly did those polling numbers really tell us? The facts may not be as clear as the Granatsteins and MacKenzies think they are.

* * *

The question of how to engage our colleagues in Quebec is frequently considered by citizen organizations, especially when several organizations come together to form a "national" coalition. Almost always, the coalition is formed by five or six English-speaking organizations headquartered in Ontario to address a particular issue or proposed legislation. At some point in the meeting, usually towards the end, someone asks, "How do we involve groups from Quebec?"

Within the ranks of campaigners in citizen organizations in Ottawa, I would guess that the ratio of English-only speakers to bilingual speakers might be roughly fifty-fifty. Regretfully, I fall into the former category. Despite the fact that I grew up in New Brunswick, Canada's only officially bilingual province, English was the language of learning in my hometown of Fredericton.

When I arrived in Ottawa in 2000, I learned quickly that being a unilingual English speaker was about as socially acceptable as being as a chain-smoker in a health club. At official or government functions where simultaneous translation is provided, unilingual English speakers are instantly "outed" when a French speaker takes the podium and some people reach for their translation earpieces. I swear there are Anglophones who would rather sit through a French presentation, politely nodding but not understanding a single word, than reach for the translation earpiece and admit they can't understand French.

When we were first setting up our missile-defence coalition, I contacted my colleague Raymond Legault in Montreal. Raymond was the head of a very successful anti-war organization called Échec à la Guerre. Like many organizations that sprang up in the lead-up to the invasion of Iraq, Échec à la Guerre was a new group, comprising local activists, students, academics, and trade unionists.

Raymond introduced me to Martine Eloy, who worked for the Quebec nurses' union. Martine was the union's representative on the anti-war coalition. Martine became our coalition's main point of contact for the Montreal group, and the only representative from Quebec on our coalition.

The first activity of our newly formed coalition, in February 2004, was the celebrity sign-on letter against missile defence. Of course, the issue quickly arose as to whether or not we would be translating our sign-on letter—and indeed all of our public documents—into French. Knowing that a professional translation cost upwards of twenty cents per word, or about a hundred dollars per page, I pointed out that translating everything could be beyond our reach financially.

One evening, early in the campaign, Martine and I spoke by phone about the best way to handle the problem. "Steve, there is a lot of language used in this sign-on letter that can't be translated for readers in Quebec," she said. "It would be easiest to start with a blank page and write a new letter against missile defence with the same demands, but written in such a way that it is meaningful to people here." She stressed that, while the English words could be exchanged for French words, what the letter needed most was a political translation.

"I think that makes a lot of sense, Martine," I replied. "You will know what kind of language and argumentation will work politically in the

Quebec context." Échec à la Guerre set about producing its own celebrity letter, which echoed the text of the English letter. As a result, we actually had a letter that could be used for both political contexts: Quebec and the "Rest-of-Canada."

I was relieved that we had found a good partner group in Quebec. It would have been impossible for us, working from outside the province, to make our campaign work in Quebec, both geographically and polit- ically.

While we in English Canada were signing up celebrities like Bryan Adams and David Suzuki, Martine and her colleagues at Échec à la Guerre were getting endorsements from singer Richard Desjardins, comedian Pascale Montpetit, feminist Françoise David, and Alexandre Trudeau, son of former prime minister Pierre Elliott Trudeau. We released both the English and the French letters on the same day.

Throughout 2004, the two campaigns continued on in parallel, one in English Canada, the other in Quebec. Each campaign had members of parliament with whom it could work closely. In our case, we stayed in regular contact with members of the NDP, the Liberals, and the Bloc Québécois. In Quebec the Bloc Québécois under Gilles Duceppe was as much opposed to Canada's participation in missile defence as the NDP, and so were many members of the Liberals' Quebec caucus.

Our campaign benefited from having Debbie Grisdale, Peggy Mason, and myself right in Ottawa; we were able to regularly trot up to Parliament Hill and meet with members of all the parties, which we did. We held many meetings with the NDP, organized by Alexa McDonough. If we had guest speakers in town, we always used the opportunity to introduce them to our friends, such as Lynn Myers, Bonnie Brown, Carolyn Parrish, and Maria Minna, in the Liberal cau- cus. We even met with a Conservative backbencher.

Our two main contacts in the Bloc Québécois were defence critic Claude Bachand and foreign-affairs critic Francine Lalonde. I first met Claude Bachand back in early 2003 when he called me up and invited me to his office. He had just read a report I had produced on Canada's military spending, and as we chatted we found we shared many opin- ions. Since then we have stayed in regular contact, and are occasionally invited to join the same panels at conferences and other gatherings.

Francine Lalonde sat on the Commons foreign affairs committee; along with Claude Bachand, she led the charge against missile defence for the Bloc Québécois in the House of Commons. The NDP's Alexa McDonough also sat on the committee, and the two of them co-operated frequently in moving issues through the committee. These two women, along with former Liberal Cabinet minister Maria Minna, co-chaired an informal, all-party group, which is called the Parliamentary Network for Nuclear Disarmament and made up of MPs concerned about international disarmament issues. The group has chapters around the world.

But to say that all of these people were "comrades in arms" would be overstating the case. They all came from different parties and their allegiances had to rest with their parties. They also came from different political cultures: the populist NDP, the centrist Liberals, and the sovereigntist yet social-democratic Bloc Québécois. The NDP and the Bloc Québécois had something in common as social democrats, but both needed to maintain a polite distance.

As non-partisan citizen groups, of course we all had to keep an identity separate from political parties while working toward the same objective of keeping Canada out of missile defence. We cultivated relationships with MPs from any party who shared our perspective, and the campaign was greatly strengthened by having political allies in Quebec.

* * *

On October 31, 2005, Hallowe'en, military historian and revered member of the defence lobby Jack Granatstein came to Ottawa to deliver the keynote address at the annual meeting of the Canadian Defence and Foreign Affairs Institute, the Calgary-based conservative think-tank.

Granatstein's topic was "Multiculturalism and Canadian Foreign Policy." He began: "I know this is a sensitive topic, which is likely why no conference has yet treated this subject. So let me play bull in the china shop." And he did.

He ploughed his way through the notion that Canada's foreign policy should be based on our desire to promote our values of peace and
development in the world. To illustrate this alarming idea, Granatstein
quoted *Globe and Mail* columnist John Ibbitson's account of the first
press conference by Canada's new governor general, Michaëlle Jean.
She spoke about the situation in Haiti as:

> reflecting a subtle but profound shift in recent Canadian polit-
> ical priorities... . The tsunami of last year, the chaos in Haiti,
> the exploding trouble in Sudan are not foreign-aid issues for
> Canada, they are foreign-policy priorities. They reflect our
> demographic transformation from predominantly European
> to truly multinational. Problems in India and China and Haiti
> are our problems because India and China and Haiti are our
> motherlands.

Granatstein rejects this perceived shift in Canadian priorities.
Instead, he thinks that our foreign policy and use of our armed forces
should not be dictated by our conscience or ethnic makeup, but by our
"national interests." In his speech, he ridiculed those who promote
Canada's role in the world as one based on altruism and values as:

> advocating policies of the heart, not policies of the head. They
> are values-oriented, not National Interest-oriented. Foreign
> Policy is not about loving everyone or even helping everyone.
> It is not about saying a nation cannot do anything, cannot go
> to war, for example, for fear of offending some group within
> the country ... For policy instead must spring from the funda-
> mental basis of a state—its geographic location, its history, its
> form of government, its economic imperatives, its alliances,
> and yes of course, its people. In other words National Interests
> are the key.

No doubt this speech was a crowd-pleaser. The Canadian Defence
and Foreign Affairs Institute, based at the University of Calgary, counts

among its fellows some of the most conservative military boosters in the country. No wonder it's backed by arms dealers and CEOs alike, including General Dynamics and the Canadian Council of Chief Executives. The Calgary crowd in the room must have particularly relished Granatstein's "blame Quebec" routine for Canada's not joining the invasion of Iraq or the Bush administration's missile shield.

"If British Canadians shaped policy on political questions in World War One and Two, French Canadians have largely shaped our defence and foreign policies since Pierre Elliot Trudeau became prime minister in 1968," argued Granatstein.

> There is no doubt—according to opinion polls—that Quebec attitudes to the military and defence spending are very cool; that Quebec attitudes to war are very different than those of English Canadians; that French Canadians' attitudes to imperialism (historically British and now U.S.) are much cooler … I would suggest that the decision to stay out of the Iraq war in 2003 was shaped by the overwhelming negative attitudes in polls in Quebec … I would suggest that the decision to refuse to join BMD in 2005 again was shaped by overwhelmingly hostile Quebec poll numbers—and by the Liberals' minority government situation.

This line that Canada did not join the invasion of Iraq or missile defence because of Quebec is generally believed by many Canadians. Even comedian Rick Mercer, after Paul Martin said Canada would not join missile defence, ran a skit on his TV program showing a missile heading for Canada from some rogue nation and the prime minister trying to defend the country by waving a poll from Quebec at it.

One of the few studies that I have found on the topic is one titled "Two Solitudes: Quebecers' Attitudes Regarding Security and Defence Policy," written by Laval University professor Jean-Sébastien Rioux (ironically, prepared for the Canadian Defence and Foreign Affairs Institute).

During the Second World War, French Canadians vociferously

opposed instituting the draft in Canada, an opposition that eventually erupted into the anti-conscription riots. Rioux argues that the origins of Quebec opinion on military matters was shaped by "the gradual formation of a unique identity for French Canadians (Canadiens) in opposition to a dual loyalty among English Canadians following Confederation. Indeed, French Canadian nationalism (and provincialism) developed in the nineteenth-century context of opposition to imperialism and to an exaggerated loyalty to Britain displayed by English Canadians."

The conscription riots themselves have become an emotional part of the Quebec identity. "Quebecers were firmly rooted in American soil and did not feel a special calling for foreign adventurism in Europe; [and felt] that the Canadian military was extremely British—French Canadians had little expectations for advancement and would only be used as cannon fodder," writes Rioux.

It certainly seems that the fact that Canada was formed by two colonial parents has greatly shaped our political culture, both inside Quebec and in the rest of Canada. It can't be overlooked that Quebec's predominant language provides it with an alternative source of information and viewpoint that the rest of Canada does not experience, and insulates it to a degree from the impact of English-language American media. Anti-Iraq-war opinion in France prior to the invasion in 2003 was very strong and was reflected in French media, which undoubtedly informed media coverage of the issue within Quebec.

But, just as one could argue that watching French television would make the viewer more dovish, one could equally argue that watching American television made the viewer more hawkish. A 2003 poll by EKOS Research found that a person's source of news had a strong influence on his or her opinion about the Canadian government's decision to not join the U.S. invasion of Iraq. Of those people who watched U.S. news, 58 percent opposed the government's anti-invasion decision and 39 percent supported it; in comparison, of those who watched Canadian news, only 22 percent opposed the government's decision and a whopping 75 percent supported staying out of Iraq.

Are missile-defence proponents overstating the importance of

Quebec public opinion in determining the government's decision to not join the U.S. missile shield?

Certainly there is a noticeable trend showing that, in polls on related issues, Quebec does typically score higher than the national average on anti-war, pro-peacekeeping questions. For instance, the results of an SES Research poll are fairly typical. In February 2003, 66 percent of Canadians felt that Canada should join the U.S. invasion of Iraq only with the approval of the United Nations, as opposed to joining a unilateral U.S. attack, while 72 percent of Quebecers felt this way. Again, 62 percent of Quebecers believed that Canada should be involved only in peacekeeping missions, and not both peacekeeping and combat missions. This was 10 points higher than the national average of 52 percent that supported peacekeeping only.

But not everyone thinks that public opinion in Quebec is as out of step with Canadian opinion as the Jack Granatsteins of the world would have us believe. Quebec researchers Stéphane Roussel and Michel Fortmann argue that Quebec opinion may be strongest, but it is in line with anti-war sentiment within Canada as a whole. In an August 2003 report entitled "Canada and the United States: An Evolving Partnership," published by the Centre for Research and Information Canada, they wrote:

> Unquestionably there is a marked difference in the way Quebecers and other Canadians view security issues. However, it is equally important to note that the *overall trends* are the same in both groups. While Quebecers' opinions may be more *pronounced* and *enduring* than those of their fellow Canadians, there is not necessarily a conflict between the viewpoints of the two groups. In fact, on most of the questions asked by pollsters, the majority of opinion in both groups clearly flows in the same direction. This is as true of relations with the United States (questions on NORTHCOM or shared values) as it is of the relevance of the UN, or its role in the crisis in Iraq. In short, the data suggest that current differences of opinion between Quebecers and other Canadians have absolutely no

bearing on the ones that divided the two communities during both world wars!

A few weeks after Prime Minister Martin decided that Canada would not join missile defence, the research firm Decima polled more than a thousand Canadians on their reaction to the government's decision. It found that a majority of Canadians supported the government's decision by a statistic landslide of 57 percent, compared with just 26 percent who opposed the decision.

While the pro-missile-defence boosters in the defence lobby and the corporate boardrooms of Bay Street were beating their chests in outrage, Canadians everywhere were quietly applauding the government. Had Paul Martin joined missile defence, according to Decima, he would have flown into a public-opinion hurricane.

The Decima poll found that every constituency in the country approved Canada's stand—teenagers to senior citizens, men and women, urban and rural dwellers. In fact, a majority in every province, including Alberta, approved of not joining Bush's missile shield. I don't know if the Jack Granatsteins of Canada realize that even a majority of the most American of all Canadian provinces, Alberta, wouldn't buy George W. Bush's missile-defence scheme. If they did, then perhaps they would all give the "blame Quebec" routine a rest.

Perhaps they are all members of one small demographic in which there was no majority in favour of staying out of missile defence: Conservative Party supporters. In this group, dominated by older Anglophone males, 49 percent were in favour of joining George W. Bush's missile shield.

These results hardly support Jack Granatstein's assertion that Quebec's pacifist preferences are holding the rest of Canada hostage. While Quebecers felt more strongly about the dangers and folly of missile defence, the sentiment stretched from coast to coast.

Maybe the divide is not so much geographical as it is political. Academics Andrew Mack and Oliver Rohlfs have argued that this is really a battle for control of our foreign policy by two groups: continentalists and internationalists.

The continentalists believe that building a stronger relationship with the United States should be Canada's first priority. "They see many of the quintessentially Canadian human security initiatives pursued by the Chrétien government as inconsequential at best, and flaky and anti-American at worst," they wrote in the *Globe and Mail* in March 2003.

Opposing the continentalists are the "beleaguered internationalists," as Mack and Rohlfs describe us, "the proponents of multilateralism and human security." The internationalists have championed initiatives from the land mines ban to the International Criminal Court—in other words, as they describe it, "much of what is distinctive about Canada's foreign policy during the past decade."

Mack and Rohlfs argue that the continentalists received a tremendous boost for their viewpoint from the terrorist attacks of September 11, 2001. "Greater defence integration and collaboration with the United States are the most effective ways to enhance Canadians' security. Their cause gained credence in the climate of fear generated by September 11. In times of crisis, the critics argue, security should begin at home."

This line of argument falls squarely in line with Granatstein's exhortation to the Canadian government to "look after the nation's interests first and values second." The part he doesn't explain is whose interests should come first, and whose values should come second.

It is fortunate for us that, when democracy works, and the will of the Canadian public is actually felt in Ottawa, Canadian values can win out over those special "interests." On the issue of missile defence the government decision was an important victory for the side of the "internationalists," wherever they live in the country.

8

STEPHEN HARPER AND BMD'S DEMISE

I was very pleased when Conservative defence critic and retired general Gordon O'Connor agreed to meet with us. It was important for the campaign to open lines of communication with all the political parties, and up until then we had had no opportunity to meet with the Conservatives. Gordon O'Connor may have accepted our invitation out of some sense of obligation one military officer has to another, for our delegation to the Conservative defence critic included our guest visitor to Ottawa, retired Lieutenant-General Robert Gard, Jr.

Before becoming the Conservative member of parliament for Carleton–Lanark, just outside of Ottawa, Gordon O'Connor had spent many years in the Canadian Forces, rising to the level of brigadier general. After his retirement in 1994, he stepped through the revolving door between the military, government, and the arms industry, and went to work for the lobby firm Hill and Knowlten Canada. He proceeded to try to win government military contracts for a list of defence companies as long as your arm. Gordon O'Connor left his work for the arms industry when he was elected to parliament in 2004.

The meeting occurred at a very important moment in the campaign—August 11, 2004, only days after the government's announcement that it was amending the NORAD agreement to allow missile-launch warning information to be shared between the Canada–U.S. global monitoring command and Northern Command, the U.S.-only command that was charged with running the American continental missile shield.

Our delegation included me, Sara Kemp, Debbie Grisdale from Physicians for Global Survival, and of course our guest, General Gard. Gordon O'Connor's office was in the MPs' office building adjacent to the Supreme Court on Wellington Street.

There we sat down at the table with Gordon O'Connor, Stockwell Day, and a younger man, who was a researcher for the party on defence issues and whom I suspected was working out of the office of Conservative Party leader Stephen Harper.

General Gard was in the midst of his very busy two-day visit to Canada at our request, dividing his time roughly evenly between meeting with MPs and speaking into media microphones. In my view, hosting people like General Gard is important not just for the media attention it draws, but for the access that such a high-level person can win for you.

Having Stockwell Day at the table was an interesting addition. We hadn't requested a meeting with him, but O'Connor's office must have invited him because, like many issues, missile defence had an impact on the departments of both National Defence and Foreign Affairs. Many Canadians' opinion of Stockwell Day had been shaped by his disastrous stint at the helm of the Reform Party's successor, the Canadian Alliance (which eventually merged with the old Progressive Conservatives to become the Conservative Party in 2003). Day's views provided an endless supply of material for political satirists, the most vulnerable of which were his ultra-conservative Christian beliefs. Rick Mercer had run a Canada-wide gender-bending petition for Stockwell to change his first name to Doris. In response to Day's professed belief in a literal interpretation of the Bible, suggesting that people must have co-existed with the dinosaurs, one Liberal commentator reminded Day that *The Flintstones* was not a documentary.

After a polite round of introductions, Gordon O'Connor stated that the Conservative Party's position on missile defence had yet to be determined, and that he was looking for more information from the government on what precisely would be Canada's role in the system.

General Gard pointed out that Canada was not needed for the system, and reiterated the argument that the system was untested and incapable of overcoming even the simplest of countermeasures that a potential enemy could use to neutralize the effectiveness of the shield. Gard distributed copies of the letter that he, along with forty-eight other retired U.S. generals and admirals, had signed and sent to President Bush. It set out their views against the system and in favour of improved security measures against demonstrable threats, such as the possibility of bombs entering the United States through a seaport.

Stockwell Day, reading the letter to Bush signed by the generals and admirals, looked up at General Gard and asked how many retired generals and admirals there were in the United States. There was an awkward pause. Was Day trying to compute the percentage of retired generals and admirals who did not sign the letter in order to minimize its significance?

General Gard replied politely that he didn't know how many retired general and admirals there were in the United States, and, with a smile, said, "I worked very hard to find my fiftieth signer for this letter, but didn't make it in time."

Day's second question was about whether a system like this would be useful if an asteroid was going to crash into the earth? Without batting an eye, Gard simply said that this system was designed to shoot down missiles and risked causing an arms race, but if we wanted a system to shoot down asteroids, that would best be done co-operatively with other countries.

The remainder of the meeting consisted of a very good exchange of information, and, after listening to Day and O'Connor, I sensed that the Conservatives were searching for a way to separate themselves from the Liberals on the missile-defence issue. They weren't prepared to just rubber-stamp joining BMD and hand all the kudos from the policy elites, the business community, and the defence lobby to Paul Martin. Instead they wanted to study the issue, hold parliamentary hearings on the terms of the deal, and even have a vote on any agreement struck between Canada and the United States.

After the meeting, Gordon O'Connor told the *Hill Times*,

We are still open minded at the moment. Our party neither supports nor rejects missile defence until we have all the details and Gen. Gard is one of the inputs but there will be a whole lot of details that we don't have yet. Gen. Gard is giving us an opinion on technology. I'd like to see some proof from the other side that it works or if it doesn't work now when will it work? What's it going to cost us? How much are we going to pay, what roles and functions are we going to be asked to do if we join it. Is the world going to be safer or less safe if we have this? What's the way we get out of it if we don't like what we get into?

The full political implication of what the Conservatives were saying did not register at first. Many media commentators continued to provide a political analysis based upon the assumption I had been going on: that the Conservatives were in favour of missile defence and would vote with the Liberals. To many Ottawa insiders, missile defence was a done deal.

Not so. The quiet young man who had sat in on that meeting with Gordon O'Connor and Stockwell Day made sure I was aware of the Conservatives' position. His name was Aaron Gairdner, and he held the post of foreign affairs and defence policy researcher in the office of the leader of the Official Opposition. He was tasked with the job of making sure the message got out that Conservative support for missile defence could not be taken for granted by the Liberals.

A few days later, Aaron sent Debbie Grisdale and me a polite e-mail thanking us for the informative meeting with General Gard. He said he wanted to make sure we were aware of the party's position, because "the fullness of the new Conservative Official Opposition policy on this developing issue may not have been completely captured by the media sound bites that you saw on TV." He was speaking of Gordon O'Connor's press conference following the August announcement that NORAD would be sharing missile-warning and assessment data with the U.S. Northern Command.

A few weeks later, Gordon O'Connor wrote an opinion piece for the *Ottawa Citizen*, entitled "Defence Planning Too Secret."

The Conservative party, at this time, neither supports nor rejects Canada's involvement in a future ballistic missile defence system. Our emphasis now is urging the government to provide Parliament with the details of the pending ballistic missile defence agreement and the foreign and defence policy context, so we can have a proper parliamentary assessment, debate and vote.

The Liberals have failed to provide Parliament with sufficient information about Canada's potential participation, while secretly entrenching Canada's role. This should be alarming to all Canadians regardless of their position on missile defence.

* * *

As the resumption of parliament in the first week of October approached, the Conservatives continued to put out the message that they would not act as a rubber stamp for the government. Each time a commentator wrote an article that made the assumption that the Conservatives would vote along with the Liberals on missile defence, Aaron would call them up to set them straight. I should know, because I made that mistake in an article I wrote, and Aaron gave me a call: "Steve, remember this is a new party, and it hasn't set a policy on this issue yet."

"Okay, yeah, I take your point," I said. "But did you see Chantal Hébert's column this week ? You've got to call her, too."

"Yes, I have already spoken to her. And David Rudd, and a few others," said Aaron.

Aaron's work was having an impact. Perhaps sensing that the Conservatives were becoming unreliable, and worried about dissension in the Liberal ranks, Defence Minister Bill Graham ratcheted up the rhetoric, and tried to sidestep the practical criticisms of missile defence by putting the issue into the context of maintaining good Canada–U.S. relations—a high priority for the government.

"There will be consequences," said Graham, if Canada did not join with the U.S. system, implying that the U.S. would use its economic clout to punish Canada. In an interview with the *Toronto Star* in late September, Graham said, "We are talking about the nature of the relationship we want with the United States ... My view is, on continental defence matters we should be really accommodating of the Americans and work with them as closely as we possibly can."

A few weeks later, Graham went a step further. "I think it is extremely dangerous for Canada to turn its back on a very important American initiative to defend ourselves and say, 'We're not going to have any part of this,'" argued Graham in the *Hill Times* on October 18, 2004.

Despite the Liberals' dire warnings, and even though it was the Cabinet's prerogative to make the decision, the government had acquiesced to opposition demands that there be a parliamentary debate and a vote on missile defence. At one point, Graham suggested that the decision could be made by Cabinet before a debate and vote was held. This elicited shouts of protests from the opposition parties, and Graham had to back down, because such a move would make any debate and a vote a farce if the decision had already been made by Cabinet.

As the resumption of parliament approached, the opposition parties kept up the pressure on missile defence. NDP leader Jack Layton said it would be "unspeakable arrogance" for Prime Minister Paul Martin to join missile defence without a vote. "Parliament must vote on whether to join Star Wars missile defence. Parliament will vote on whether to join Star Wars missile defence," Layton told a public forum at Carleton University.

Parliament resumed in the first week of October 2004 and missile defence was at the top of the political agenda. All eyes were on the Martin government and how it was going to manoeuvre the missile-defence file through a minority parliament. It didn't take long for the Liberals to learn that the Conservatives had plans of their own on missile defence.

A few days after the Liberals' Throne Speech, which set out the government's agenda for the coming session, the Conservatives put forward their own response, including how missile defence should be handled. "We need to know clearly the objective of this initiative," Stephen Harper told parliament on October 6, "whether it is technically feasible, exactly what role Canada would play, as well as the potential costs and benefits, [and] the nature and length of any Canadian commitments."

Harper put forward the basis of an amendment to the Liberals' Throne Speech, composed of five proposals, including tax cuts and the creation of several commissions—but most importantly, a vote on Canadian participation in missile defence.

The NDP's initial reaction was very cool. Jack Layton accused the Conservatives of playing "political chicken," because, if an amendment passed without the Liberals' support, it could be considered a vote of "non-confidence," and the Liberal minority government would fall. The Conservatives would benefit, because they would be asked to form a government, or else Canadians would be faced with another election.

But it soon became clear that it was not the intention of the Conservatives to bring down the government, but rather to remind Paul Martin that he could not govern as if he had a majority; he had to listen to the demands of the opposition parties. A compromise was eventually reached, and all four parties voted in favour of a series of amendments a few weeks later.

The final changes to the Throne Speech included this very important phrase: "with respect to an agreement on ballistic missile defence, the assurance that Parliament will have an opportunity to consider all public information pertaining to the agreement and to vote prior to a government decision."

This political move on missile defence by the Conservatives was unexpected. They were essentially establishing a very high bar for Paul Martin to get over—but it was not insurmountable. To win the support of the Conservatives, Martin had to bring to parliament a missile-defence Memorandum of Understanding (MOU), negotiated between Canada and the United States. This was significant because MOUs between the United States and other countries that joined the missile shield, such as Australia and the United Kingdom, had never been made public (although the U.K.'s MOU was leaked).

The MOU would then be the subject of an intense debate. The Liberals would have to demonstrate that it was in Canada's interest to sign the missile-defence deal. Specifically, Martin would have to show that Canada had influence in the operation of the missile shield, that NORAD was protected, that the system would not require Canadian territory or money, and that Canadian industry would benefit from U.S. contracts to build the system.

There was one additional condition: that the shield would not result in weapons being put in space. The Liberals had made it clear that they believed that the system would not use space weapons, and when negotiations officially commenced in June 2003, and the defence minister at the time, John McCallum, said that Canada's participation hinged on this fact.

But some observers noted that, in January 2004, Defence Minister David Pratt had quietly dropped Canada's opposition to space weapons in pursuing more formalized negotiations with the United States. Nevertheless, the government continued to profess its opposition to the weaponization of space and argued that the missile-shield plan did not include space weapons.

Now, with the Conservatives' amendment, the government was committed to bringing an agreement before parliament. How could Paul Martin show that the United States agreed with Canada's analysis that space weapons would not be used as part of the missile shield? Could he get agreement from the Americans to put a "no space weapons" commitment in the terms of a deal with Canada?

The Conservatives didn't want to scuttle Canada joining missile defence, but their Throne Speech amendment had that effect. How ironic it is that the party most likely to desire closer relations to the United States, and the one most comfortable with military matters, may have inadvertently set up the conditions that made it impossible for the Liberals to join the U.S. missile defence program.

The amendment forced Martin to negotiate a missile-defence deal that could survive close public scrutiny. The deal had to meet all of the expectations that Martin had raised about Canada's participation— from Canada having influence over the system to the Americans giv-

STEPHEN HARPER AND BMD'S DEMISE

ing up the possible use of space weapons. Not only did it have to pass public scrutiny, but the Conservatives had to support the deal as well, and vote in favour of it, in order for it to pass through the minority parliament.

It was a tall order for Paul Martin to deliver—especially considering his own party was divided over the issue and public opinion was moving against missile defence. *Toronto Star* columnist Chantal Hébert put it like this: "Given a choice between greatly embarrassing themselves with the American administration of the day or with Canadian voters in general, which would Prime Minister Paul Martin and his minority government choose?"

It was clear that, with each passing month, the more Paul Martin delayed making a decision on missile defence the more difficult—and costly—that decision became.

* * *

Of course we were very pleased that missile defence had become the hottest issue in Ottawa by late 2004. Paul Martin's promise to hold a vote added a new political wrinkle to the issue. With a deal put on the table for a debate, we could investigate and discuss the exact nature of Canada's participation—something that had not been determined so far. As well, a minority government meant that every backbench MP's vote was important to the government. Each member had to make his or her own decision on missile defence; every vote was important and could not be taken for granted.

For the opposition parties, the prospect of a missile-defence vote was a political lever they could use on the Liberal government. A vote could wrench open the divisions in the Liberal Party, which in previous votes had seen nearly forty members vote against missile defence, against the wishes of the prime minister. As one commentator put it, missile defence could pass with more Conservatives voting for it than Liberals.

But as the calls for a vote from opposition parties became louder and louder throughout late August, September, and October, those of us leading the campaign became somewhat worried. It seemed that the political objective of actually preventing Canada from joining missile defence was slipping into a political game, in which embarrassing the Liberals had become the chief objective. Demanding a vote on missile defence too soon could be a rush to defeat for the campaign.

In late August, Jack Layton emerged from a meeting with Prime Minister Martin pledging to press the missile-defence issue. "We intend to press this issue very hard. The prime minister understood that we would be doing that," Layton told reporters after the meeting. "It's a minority parliament and our position on the issue is very clear, as I think it is the position of most of the other parties. Within the Liberal Party, there seem to be some differences between some of the members."

The day after Jack made those comments, some of our campaign strategists met. We were worried that it would be unwise to push Martin for an early vote on Canada and BMD before the U.S. presidential election on November 2, 2004, because, if there were a vote right now, the pro-BMD side would have won.

We decided to raise the issue with Alexa, and later she agreed with our concerns. Calling for a vote was fine—but not an early vote. We at least had to see what was going to happen with the U.S. election. Later, a delegation met with the Bloc Québécois's foreign-affairs critic, Francine Lalonde, and we passed on to her our concern that an early vote on missile defence would not help our cause. She also agreed, and said she would raise it with party leader Gilles Duceppe. We seemed to have both the NDP and the BQ on side, and we hoped this meant that neither party would introduce their own motion to rush a missile-defence vote.

But, as the weeks passed, Jack Layton's demands for a vote did not seem to abate at all. Our allies in the Liberal backbenches were becoming worried too. They said that Paul Martin's office was putting a lot of pressure on them to drop their objections to missile defence, and they all felt that a vote would not be a good strategy at the moment because it would only increase the pressure on them. The *Hill Times* ran an informal survey of MPs on whether there should be a vote on missile defence, and every single Liberal MP that we knew was opposed to missile defence said that there should not be a vote.

At midnight on October 17, 2004, I typed out an e-mail message to Jack Layton's BlackBerry from my home. "Dear Jack," I wrote:

> Alexa has made a compelling case to us in the past that a missile-defence vote is undesirable because the Conservatives would join with the Liberal Cabinet and parliamentary secretaries to pass a motion. That's why I and others have been confused by your calls for a vote—which our side would surely lose ... There is a consensus that we should continue to stall, as a delay in a Cabinet decision works in our favour. One such tactic would be to call for public hearings on missile defence before any vote in the House, and of course before any decision by the Cabinet.

The next morning my cell phone rang as I was getting ready to leave for the office. On the other end was Jamey Heath, the NDP's director of communications and research, and Jack's closest political adviser. He had obviously received the e-mail I sent to Jack. Jamey and I spoke for about twenty minutes, and I could hear a sense of frustration in his voice. "Missile defence is a done deal, Steve," Jamey said.

"No, I disagree, Jamey," I said. "But if you act like it is, it will become a self-fulfilling prophecy."

The situation was becoming clear to me. Jamey thought that we had already lost the issue, and so his strategy was based on making it as painful as possible for Martin to join missile defence. It was Jamey's job to be strictly partisan in his strategy; his first priority was to help the party as much as possible—and occasionally, as the logic of partisan politics goes, losing an issue would be more helpful to the NDP than winning. If Martin made such a politically unpopular decision as joining George W. Bush's "Star Wars," then all the more people would vote NDP in the next election.

"Look, remember that you and I got into this business because of the issues, right?" I said to Jamey, trying to appeal to the same sense of social justice that I knew we shared but pursued in different ways—he inside the system and I outside. "No one is saying drop your demand for a vote. Just don't ask for an *early* vote," I implored him. "Can we shift focus to public hearings perhaps, so we can keep up the pressure on the government without ending the campaign prematurely?"

This was one of those moments when strategies diverge. Political parties and social movements are different political animals, but as long as communication is taking place, it is possible to find strategies that work for both. Jamey was going to take that back to the other strategists and Jack, but I felt I had convinced him.

Later that day I received a second call on my cell phone; this time it was Jack Layton himself. "Steve, we're going to call for public hearings on missile defence. Thanks for staying in touch," said Jack. He said that the amendment to the Throne Speech also contained the commitment that "Parliament will have an opportunity to consider all public information pertaining to the agreement." And the NDP would argue that this could be interpreted to mean public hearings. I told him we would support the party's position and encourage others to do the same.

The NDP put the strategy into play right away. On Monday Alexa McDonough submitted a notice of motion to the Commons Foreign Affairs Committee, of which she was a member. It called on the committee "not to sign any memorandum of understanding or treaty that entrenches Canada's formal participation in the U.S. Ballistic Missile Defence plan until public hearings in every province and territory on the matter are concluded and a report with recommendations is tabled in Parliament."

Once again, we wound up our Internet system and encouraged our thousands of supporters to go to our Ceasefire.ca Web site to send their own letter to the members of the all-party committee, urging them to support the NDP's motion. E-mails flooded into the committee members' offices within a few days. On Thursday, the day of the committee meeting, the Conservatives' lead representative on the committee complained on CBC Radio that he had received "hundreds of e-mails" demanding public hearings.

Liberal representative Dan McTeague added that "you can't have a public consultation on a matter the public doesn't even understand yet." The Liberals and the Conservatives voted together against the

NDP and the Bloc Québécois to defeat Alexa's motion. Alexa told CBC, "Canadians demand and expect to be consulted on this incredibly important decision ... Parliament is not the centre of the universe."

* * *

If Democratic presidential candidate John Kerry had beaten incumbent Republican George W. Bush and won the 2004 U.S. election, Canada would be a full partner in ballistic missile defence today.

This is the direct opposite of what some would have expected—that a Kerry victory would have let Canada off the hook. After all, John Kerry was no great fan of missile defence. While not totally opposed to it, Kerry pledged to reduce its funding and use the money for other purposes, such as recruiting more troops. Wouldn't this have given Paul Martin an "out" on missile defence?

Not really, because Martin wanted to join. This is more likely: if John Kerry had won the election, much of the opposition to missile defence would have crumbled, because Canadians would have felt that Kerry would not use the system for offensive purposes, and would likely not put weapons into space or provoke the Russians and the Chinese. Having Kerry in the White House instead of George W. Bush would have made joining the system more palatable for Canadians.

No doubt this is what Paul Martin and his circle of missile defence supporters were hoping for. In fact, the decision to amend the NORAD agreement in the summer of 2004 was likely a way to buy time until the U.S. presidential election was held on November 2, 2004.

A few days before the U.S. election, *Toronto Star* columnist Jim Travers described Martin's dilemma like this:

> Paul Martin and his key advisors have their fingers crossed that a moderate Democrat in the White House, particularly one roughly aligned with this country on nuclear proliferation, will make it easier for Canadians to support the missile plan ...

> Their optimism is rooted in pessimism. A government wary of the implications of not joining the program is having little

luck convincing the country, let alone a recalcitrant Liberal caucus, to shelter under the missile umbrella.

What's worse for the Martin government is that the once rock solid Conservatives are wavering. Now, with seats to protect in Ontario and others they want to win in Quebec, Stephen Harper's reconstituted right-of-centre party has worked through the same equation as the Liberals and reached the similar conclusion that unequivocal backing for missile defence is not politically astute ...

Martin's challenge is getting Canadians to grasp that it would be smart to support something so patently foolish. In practical political terms, that means trying to close the gap between what the country wants to do and what the government is convinced must be done.

Unfortunately, it was not to be. On November 3, 2004, the world awoke to four more years of George W. Bush. Another door was slammed shut for the Canadian government on missile defence. No doubt Prime Minister Paul Martin was regretting having put off a decision for so long. A Kerry victory would probably have presented the last chance he had to bring Canada into missile defence without tearing his own party apart and bleeding support the next time he had to go to the polls. The writing was on the wall: missile defence was in serious trouble.

To the surprise of many observers, President Bush accepted an invitation to visit Ottawa from the prime minister during Martin's post-election congratulatory call. In fact, the president put the visit at the top of his schedule, and would make his first official visit to Canada on November 30 and December 1, 2004. Bush was planning on an important tour of European capitals early in 2005 to rebuild transatlantic relations strained by the controversial invasion of Iraq, and his visit to Canada would be his first stop on this goodwill tour.

The missile-defence lobby went into overdrive to push Martin to make a decision on missile defence now that the outcome of the U.S. election was known and President Bush would be visiting Canada soon. But instead, Paul Martin continued to delay and downplayed expectations that he and Bush would even be discussing missile defence during the two-day visit.

According to Mike Duffy, a journalist with CTV, Defence Minister Bill Graham had suggested wrapping the missile-defence decision into the Canada–U.S. NORAD agreement, due for renewal in May 2006— more than a year later.

The *Globe and Mail* quoted a government source as saying the government was not coming under pressure from the Bush administration: "Do we get the sense from the Americans that Canada has to do something on missile defence ten minutes ago? No, we don't," the *Globe and Mail* quoted the unidentified source as saying.

U.S. ambassador to Canada, Paul Cellucci, in his book *Unquiet Diplomacy,* expressed his frustration at not being able to make an announcement on a missile-defence deal: "To my great disappointment, we couldn't even get the issue onto the formal agenda for the talks between the president and the prime minister. Two years of off-and-on negotiations and we still had to keep up the pretence that this was not a vitally important issue between us."

* * *

On November 30, 2004, Air Force One touched down at the Ottawa International Airport. The presidential motorcade whisked President Bush and his wife, Laura, to the Lester B. Pearson Building on the banks of the Ottawa River, the home of the Department of Foreign Affairs. They conveniently avoided the thousands of protesters that filled the streets of downtown Ottawa.

Prime Minister Martin and President Bush held three meetings. They talked about security and border issues for forty-five minutes with officials present, and then discussed trade and economic issues during a working lunch, according to the *Toronto Star.* In another forty-five-minute meeting, Bush and Martin were joined by National Security Advisor Condoleezza Rice and Jonathan Freid, Martin's foreign-policy adviser.

But despite its not being on the official agenda, President Bush raised the missile-defence issue with the prime minister.

According to Ambassador Paul Cellucci, Bush pressed the issue "because he couldn't understand what the basis was for the Canadian government's reluctance to sign on to missile defence, particularly after the amendment to NORAD the previous summer. Like me, the president saw it as being in Canada's sovereign and national interests to participate"

Later, a White House source told Canadian Press that Bush did not intend to strong-arm Martin. "[President Bush] took a conciliatory message to Canada about moving beyond Iraq and moving forward." In his defence, Prime Minister Martin explained that he was in a minority government and, while the decision rested with him and his Cabinet, he had agreed to a debate and vote in parliament on the issue. According to some reports, Martin fingered Stephen Harper for withholding support for the Liberals on missile defence.

The Canadian ambassador to the United States, Michael Kergin, who was present in the meeting, said that he did not feel that Bush pressured Martin. "The president, from my very clear recollection, said, 'I believe in the system [and] I don't quite understand why Canadians have a phobia about it," Mr. Kergin told Canadian Press.

Kergin added that Paul Martin told President Bush that Canadians were concerned that the system would ultimately cause an arms race in space. "Mr. Martin said, 'We are concerned about the weaponization of space,' said Kergin." But President Bush would not give any assurance that space weapons would not be part of the system in the future. "This is land-based and sea-based. [But] the military is never going to rule out anything," Bush said, according to Kergin.

But the *Washington Post* reported an unidentified Canadian source as saying that Bush "leaned across the table and said: 'I'm not taking this position, but some future president is going to say: Why are we paying to defend Canada?'"

Like Bush, Paul Cellucci didn't accept Martin's defence either.

Well, there had already been two votes on motions tabled by

the [Canadian] Alliance and the Bloc [Québécois] and those opposed to missile defence had been pretty solidly thumped on both occasions. We could all do the arithmetic. Even if all the BQ and NDP members voted against missile defence, joined by 30 or even 40 Liberals, a third vote on missile defence would still pass if all the Conservatives voted for it.

Following the meeting, the two leaders emerged for a photo opportunity and a press conference. As Paul Cellucci put it, "President Bush decided it was time for him to do a bit of public diplomacy." Bush thanked Canadians for the warm welcome and paid tribute to Canada's contributions in Afghanistan and Haiti, but then, as *Globe and Mail* columnist Jeffrey Simpson described it, Bush, "slid a knife into Mr. Martin's ribs."

"We talked about the future of NORAD," said Bush to the assembled journalists and photographers, "and how that organization can best meet emerging threats and safeguard our continent against attack from ballistic missiles." Martin reportedly looked very uncomfortable.

The journalists present were caught completely off guard by Bush's missile-defence comment. As incredible as it may seem, not one reporter asked a single question about missile defence in response to Bush's obvious invitation to discuss the issue. Apparently, the handful of reporters selected from amongst the National Press Gallery to attend the press conference with the president were so confident that missile defence would not be raised that they had not prepared any questions on the subject and did not generate any on the spot. "It was appalling" that no one picked up on the issue, one Hill reporter, who was not at the press conference, said to me later that day.

But Bush was not finished. He had another important meeting that day, at which he intended to discuss missile defence, and it was with Conservative Party leader Stephen Harper. Months later it was discovered by Canadian Press that Bush "scolded" Harper for his silence on missile defence and asked him to help secure Canadian involvement in the U.S. plan.

According to an unnamed U.S. source, Bush said to Harper, "Please don't play partisan politics with this. I would hope you're looking at this in Canada's national interest and not in terms of partisan politics."

Stephen Harper did not deny being pressured by Bush, but defended himself, saying that the president had been misinformed by someone about Conservative policy. "It was clear to me at the outset of our conversation that the president had been misinformed about our position," said Harper. "We're not going to agree to a proposal we don't have the details for," he said. "Let's see [the Liberals] govern and make a decision for once, instead of relying on us."

The next day, December 1, 2004, President Bush flew to Halifax, where he was confronted by thousands more peaceful demonstrators, organized by the Halifax Peace Coalition. He delivered his keynote address in Canada at the historic Pier 21, where he raised Canada's involvement in missile defence for a second time publicly. "I hope we will move forward on ballistic-missile defence co-operation, to protect the next generation of Canadians and Americans from the threats we know will arise," Bush said.

Back in our offices in Ottawa, we cheered at the news that President Bush had not once, but twice now, raised missile defence. There is a saying that I often recall that goes something like this: "Do not what you wish to do the most, but what your opponent wishes you to do the least." In this case, the last thing Paul Martin wanted was George W. Bush to come to Canada and publicly ask Canada to join missile defence. Like Martin, we knew that a large number of Canadians would oppose missile defence simply because this unpopular U.S. president wanted us to join.

President Bush's visit to Canada at the beginning of December was the final nail in the coffin for Canada joining missile defence. In the months that followed, the government slid steadily toward its "no" decision on February 24, 2005, for reasons explored in the last chapter.

Of course the Conservatives wailed over the government's decision, and accused the Liberals of misleading the Americans, abandoning Canada's continental security responsibilities, and the like. But not all missile-defence proponents joined in the Conservatives' denunciation of the Liberals for dropping the ball. In fact, many quite properly pointed out that Stephen Harper had to shoulder some of the blame for Canada not joining missile defence.

Even before Bush's visit, the conservative *National Post* had raised the alarm about Stephen Harper's leadership. In an editorial provocatively entitled "Does Canada Have a Conservative Party?" *National Post* editorialists wrote, "Mr. Harper is shifting the party to the mushy middle ... Yesterday it was reported the party is backing away from its support for Canadian participation in a missile defence shield."

The day after Bush's visit, the *National Post* said Harper had much to learn from Bush's political instincts. Like Bush, Stephen Harper "needs to start speaking out more forcefully on subjects of concern to conservative Canadian voters ... In the past few months, Mr. Harper has soft-pedaled tax cuts, endorsed the Liberals' massive increase in health care spending and dodged questions over whether his party endorses Canada's participation in the U.S. missile defence program."

In a testy letter to the newspaper, Harper shot back: "In our meeting last week, President Bush and I did indeed discuss conservatism. I was able to tell him that Canada most certainly had a conservative party. What it lacks is a national conservative newspaper."

After the decision to not participate was announced, the *Calgary Sun* ran an editorial saying that Canada opted out of ballistic missile defence because of Conservative opposition. Again, Harper wrote back that "this is without foundation."

Criticism of Harper came not just from Conservative backers, but from pro-missile-defence Liberals as well. Senator Colin Kenny wrote in the *Ottawa Citizen*:

Do I feel that Paul Martin let me down? No, I feel that Stephen Harper let the country—and his party—down ...

Stephen Harper decided to sell out his beliefs and values for a mess of pottage in Quebec. I've talked to a lot of Conservatives, both in the House and the Senate, and just about every one of them told me the same thing: There aren't many Conservatives on Parliament Hill who don't believe that Canadian participation would have been a good idea.

But Harper is desperate to pick up seats in Quebec in the next election—a most unlikely prospect.

The man who long denounced Liberals as being value-free opportunists showed himself to be not just the biggest opportunist around, but also a man willing to trade a lot for the prospect of very little.

That takes him beyond opportunism, into the realm of stupidity.

So it is on this point that I am in the strange position of agreeing with both the *National Post* and Senator Colin Kenny that it was the Conservatives and their unreliable support for the Liberals that was a major factor in Paul Martin's calculation that he had nowhere left to turn. He had to reverse his position, and say "no" to missile defence.

But ultimately, it was the fact that the Canadian public did not want to be part of Bush's system that won the day. Our campaign had achieved what all citizen-based campaigns aspire to do, and that is to pull public opinion and begin to tilt the entire political system to your point of view. If we still live in a democracy, the theory goes, then all political parties will follow the voters. Certainly the Conservatives were reading the same polls as the Liberals, and they could not afford to be on the wrong side of Canadian popular opinion on (another) issue— no matter how angry their Conservative base became with them.

9

NOWHERE LEFT TO TURN

It was a wonderful irony. On December 1, 2004, all the TV networks were geared up, ready to transmit U.S. President George W. Bush's keynote speech from his podium on Pier 21 in Halifax into millions of Canadian living rooms. Bush's message for Canada? "I hope we will move forward on ballistic missile defence co-operation."

But that is not how it happened. Instead, another newsworthy event overtook the president's speech and meant that George W. Bush's prime-time moment would have to wait. That night, CBC-TV led its newscast with news of the death of one of Canada's most celebrated authors and nationalists, Pierre Berton. Instead of Bush's rallying cry for his War on Terrorism, Canadians were reminded of the life of a great Canadian who had devoted himself to telling us that we had our own history and our own place in the world.

What made this conjunction of events even more ironic is the fact that one of the last political acts Pierre Berton took was to add his name to our "Stars Against Star Wars" letter earlier in the year. If it hadn't been for his failing health, he told our organizer Jillian Skeet, he would have gladly joined us at our press conference to release that letter to the media.

The next morning, I was on a plane headed for Victoria, British Columbia, to take part in a citizens' forum on Canada–U.S. "deep integration" organized by the Council of Canadians. The forum was part of a series being held across the country, and this particular event was focusing on missile defence. I was to present my view on the issue to the audience and a panel of commissioners composed of the council's chairperson, Maude Barlow, former head of the Canadian Union of Public Employees Judy Darcy, and long-time peace activist and physician Mary-Wynne Ashford.

I delivered a presentation that I had been developing over the previous weeks, first to a meeting of the Canadian Pugwash Group in Toronto and later at a conference organized by the Doukhobors at Castlegar in the British Columbia interior. Each time I gave the speech, I became more optimistic that we could actually win this campaign to keep Canada out of missile defence. It was as if I was convincing myself every time I delivered the reasons why we could win.

As I told my audiences, I could see the political stars and planets lining up in a way that favoured our final achievement of the goal we had set out many months before—of moving Paul Martin to say "no" on missile defence.

Here's why:

Paul Martin stirred up nationalist sentiment in the election campaign, limiting his ability to pursue something as unpopular and U.S.-friendly as joining missile defence.

The minority government and dissension in his own party gave Paul Martin very little room to manoeuvre, and forced him to agree to a vote in parliament, where two opposition parties were four-square against missile defence.

The NORAD amendment in the summer had secured the future of the prized joint U.S.–Canada command without requiring Canada to join missile defence.

Missile defence was causing serious divisions and discord in his party, already damaged by infighting between the Chrétien and Martin camps.

The Conservatives forced Paul Martin to deliver on his promises in writing by insisting a deal be put before parliament on a vote, in spite of the fact that some of those promises, such as preventing the weaponization of space, might be impossible to deliver.

Polls were now showing consistent and growing opposition to missile defence, which reached 56 percent nationally and a majority in every region by late October (before Bush won the election).

The re-election of George W. Bush and his ill-considered missile-defence statements during his official Canadian visit linked Canadians' antipathy to Bush with Canada's involvement in missile defence.

But most importantly, sitting there on the plane to Victoria, I was clutching a news clipping from the *Vancouver Sun* from November 15, 2004. It was written by reporter Peter O'Neil and bore the headline "Martin Downplays Ottawa's Support for 'Star Wars' Missile Defence System."

The day it appeared, Sara had come into the office holding the clipping and said, "This is how it's going to end, Steve. He's going to say he'll focus on the Canadian North instead of missile defence."

According to the story, Martin had emerged from yet another raucous meeting with Liberal Party members in Penticton, B.C., and said missile defence wasn't a top national-security issue: "My focus now is on the defence of North America, and that's our coasts, it's our Arctic sovereignty, and that's where we're going to put the concentration."

Martin added that the NORAD amendment was the most significant step. "That was a crucial decision for Canada." The prime minister's comment suggested that he felt that the NORAD agreement had bought him time. As he said,

> There's an enormous amount of research involved in [a decision], and what is of greatest interest to me right now is to monitor the situation and to follow it, and we will continue discussing with the Americans.

> But the priority is what we can do now in the fight against terrorism, in the protection of our borders, in the protection of our coasts in making sure we have the intelligence information that we require to defend Canada.

At the Penticton meeting, a motion against missile defence that had been introduced by the Young Liberals of B.C. was chosen as a "priority resolution" by B.C. members for debate at the Liberal Party national convention scheduled for March 2005 in Ottawa.

This meant that the anti-missile-defence resolution would go to an open debate and vote on the floor, setting up missile defence as the most high-profile, and contentious, issue at the convention.

It was as if Paul Martin saw the train wreck that awaited him: a bitter internal fight that would erupt into a heated debate, involving not just his caucus but the entire Liberal Party in a very public feud in front of the national news media. Paul Martin knew that opinion in his own party largely reflected national public opinion as a whole—which meant that he could expect to lose the debate and have the party pass a resolution against missile defence.

While the motion from the party would be non-binding on the government, it would be very divisive, and humiliating for the prime minister himself. Frankly, Paul Martin must have been wondering what advantage was left to him in pursuing missile defence.

During my presentation in Victoria I put my analysis forward: if people looked closely at the signs, they could see that it was possible for us to win the campaign. But my optimism was greeted coolly by some skeptics in the audience. One woman repeated what I had heard many times before: "It's a done deal." She questioned whether anything people did would make any difference.

I have to admit there was a shadow of doubt in my own mind. Maybe I was just inflating the significance of these statements, searching for some positive news. The *Vancouver Sun* article appeared in only a handful of newspapers, and Martin had not repeated the remarks since. Was it wishful thinking on my part? Was I seeing signs that weren't really there?

Despite the fact that I may have sounded like a naïve Pollyanna, I felt that, if our own supporters believed the struggle was hopeless, then we would certainly lose in the end. We needed to keep up the pressure, and that meant people having enough hope to keep them writing letters, collecting signatures on petitions, participating in events, and engaging in other actions.

"If it's a done deal," I said, "and Canada had already signed some secret agreement and the United States, say, really was satisfied with that change to the NORAD agreement, then tell me why George W. Bush flew all the way to Canada and, ignoring all the advice given to him by his advisers, publicly asked Canada to join missile defence?"

Clearly, Bush was not satisfied with the change to NORAD or any secret agreement. He didn't really need Canadian territory or money. The most valuable contribution we could make was Canada's political endorsement of the system. Then George W. Bush could show his critics at home and around the world that even Canada the peacekeeper, Canada the advocate of banning landmines, Canada the champion of nuclear disarmament, embraced his missile-defence system.

So it was the political endorsement of missile defence that we had to deny George W. Bush. The NORAD agreement was a step in the wrong direction, but it was not the same as joining missile defence. We needed Paul Martin to say "no" to George W. Bush and deny him the political cover that he sought for his missile scheme.

* * *

As the campaign progressed, we regularly analyzed the political moment and evaluated our strategy. We checked back on three scenarios we had set out in March 2004. In the first scenario we staved off a government decision to join BMD, in the second scenario we limited participation by forcing Paul Martin to set caveats on Canada's role, and in the third scenario we actually forced Paul Martin to say no to joining missile defence.

Using these three scenarios as a reference point, in late 2004, we concluded that the campaign was moving from the first scenario to the second. For instance, the NORAD decision in the summer was clearly an effort to buy time and delay a decision until after the U.S. election. But after his victory, Bush made a major strategic error by ignoring his own advisers and raising missile defence in Canada during his official visit. Martin's defence against this was to start setting limits on what any potential agreement could include, such as no money for the system, no territory for interceptors, and other caveats. Attitudes were hardening against missile defence, not just in the general public but in Martin's own caucus. Martin was forced to respond by being seen to resist perceived pressure from Bush to join.

A few weeks after Bush's visit to Canada, Doug Roche contacted me and asked what I thought could be done to keep the political pressure on Martin. I replied that our strategy was—as before—threefold: political, communications, and organizing.

Our political strategy included a plan for each political party: strengthen resistance in the Liberal backbenches, support the NDP's daily interventions in the House, stay in contact with the Bloc and make use of their working relationship and influence with the Conservatives, and find at least one Conservative backbencher who would come out publicly against missile defence.

Our communications strategy now included improving our ability to produce and place influential opinion pieces in daily news media, and continuing to bring experts to Ottawa to speak to the media and MPs, just as we did with retired General Gard.

Finally, our updated organizing strategy sought to build pressure at the riding level on MPs for the anticipated free vote on missile defence, through letter-writing campaigns and demonstrations directed toward local MPs. In addition, we were setting out plans to influence the Liberal and Conservative party conventions that were planned for March 2005.

Based on the success of General Gard's visit, we organized several more visits by people whom we felt would be persuasive messengers for our arguments against missile defence. It was an incredibly effective strategy, because these experts' arguments were carried widely by the media, and we used their visits as opportunities to meet with members of parliament and build more political connections.

As the year drew to a close, the public momentum had moved to our side of the argument. The missile-defence lobby was becoming alarmed at our success. The *Globe and Mail* ran another pro-missile-defence editorial just before the Bush visit, this one titled "It's Decision Time on Missile Defence."

NOWHERE LEFT TO TURN

Before the June election, Prime Minister Paul Martin was leery of missile defence for fear it might cost him the nationalist vote. Now he's jittery because President George W. Bush is soon coming to Ottawa, and signing on to the controversial program might look like servility.

Enough. The Prime Minister has been wedged on the fence for months. He should decide. Contrary to the ranting of the Canadian left, this is no dark Bushite conspiracy to take over the continent. But here's a novel idea: Mr. Martin could lead. He could make the hard-headed pragmatic and idealistic arguments for joining missile defence, persuade his caucus and the nation, and dare Conservative Stephen Harper to say no. What's he waiting for?

To our surprise, underscoring the growing divide between pubic opinion and the media elites, even the left-leaning *Toronto Star* came out in favour of missile defence. "Canada has a responsibility to help the U.S. defend North American cities against attack by a rogue state like North Korea or against an accidental launch. The North Atlantic Treaty Organization has endorsed exploring missile defences. Why should Canada boycott what is essentially a high-tech research program?" wrote the *Star* in a profoundly misinformed editorial. Later, the ultra-conservative *National Post* would congratulate its progressive rival in Toronto for seeing the wisdom of missile defence.

We pressed on with an intense communications and lobbying campaign. In October we had hosted Ottawa meetings and media events with author Mel Hurtig, MIT scientist Ted Postol, and Université du Québec physicist Louis Marchildon. In November, we hosted British Labour MP Alan Simpson.

We piled on the arguments against joining missile defence: it would undermine Canadian sovereignty, it didn't work, opposition existed in the United States and even in British military and political establishments. But the system's relationship to space weapons emerged as one of the most damning arguments against missile defence. Canadians did not trust President Bush and worried that he planned to use the system to put weapons into space.

We built on this concern by inviting former ambassador Jonathan Dean to visit Ottawa from Washington. Dean was a retired American disarmament negotiator and was working with the Union of Concerned Scientists. His organization had produced very strong research linking missile defence to space weapons, and even argued that the existing ground-based system could be used to destroy other countries' satellites, making the system a prohibited anti-satellite weapon.

A grant from the Arsenault Family Foundation in Colorado provided enough funds to cover the cost of Dean's trip to Canada.

In late November I spoke by phone to Ambassador Dean at his Washington, D.C., office: "Ambassador, we need you to come to Ottawa to deliver a message: that missile defence will weaponize space. And maybe that message could quite literally be a letter to the prime minister from your organization. We could explain that you are here in Canada to deliver an open letter to the prime minister, warning him that the U.S. plans to deploy weapons in space and to use the existing system as an anti-satellite weapon system. Would you be willing to do that?"

He agreed to consult with his staff about what would be most appropriate for his organization, and we set to work preparing for Ambassador Dean's visit. As we had done with high-profile guests before, we filled his few days in Ottawa with media interviews and meetings with MPs. On the first day of his visit, he and I, along with Peggy Mason and Debbie Grisdale, stood together at a well-attended press conference in the Parliament Buildings. The press conference was carried live across Canada on CTV's all-news channel, Newsnet. The fact that CTV carried the press conference for more than fourteen uninterrupted minutes underscores the level of interest in the issue.

"Our analysis clearly shows that the missile defense system currently being fielded will not provide protection against long-range ballistic missile attacks," said the letter to Prime Minister Martin written by Dean and the president of the Union of Concerned Scientists, David C. Wright.

"It seems to me that the trend in missile defence is inevitably into the space component, and one will lead to another," Dean said.

After the press conference, as we were milling about in the room,

chatting with the reporters present, I noticed a photographer was posing Ambassador Dean for a photograph. The next morning, I opened
the *Globe and Mail* and couldn't believe my eyes. There, on page four,
below the headline "Arms Experts Issue Missile-Defence Alert," was
that photograph, covering almost half of the page. It was a skillfully
arranged shot of Ambassador Dean holding his open letter to the
prime minister up to the camera, and it was so large one could read the
text of the letter.

In the span of two days, Ambassador Dean and our delegation met
eighteen MPs individually or in groups; this included a private meeting with a Conservative member who opposed missile defence, and a
formal presentation to the House of Commons Standing Committee
on Foreign Affairs and International Trade.

NDP leader Jack Layton attended an early-morning meeting with a
group of MPs who were members of the non-partisan international
group Parliamentarians Network for Nuclear Disarmament.

Later I received an e-mail from Jamey Heath. "You guys got some
good coverage on Dean today. Congrats. They are in deep, deep trouble on this issue," wrote Jamey, and he attached a transcript of Jack
Layton's comments during Question Period in the House.

Layton had said, "Today we learned that the Union of Concerned
Scientists, with arms experts and people who know this material inside
and out, are ratifying and confirming what the criticisms of the arms
race have been all along. Missile defence is going to increase the
buildup of arms globally. It is going to lead to the weaponization of
space, and it is going to take away from Canada's credibility in arguing
for disarmament."

To a degree the *Globe and Mail* was correct that Martin was avoiding
taking the lead in making the case for missile defence. Defence
Minister Bill Graham carried the argument for joining missile defence
almost single-handedly for the government, while we kept repeating
our messages through a combination of expert visitors, op-eds, letters
to the editor, and even well-timed demonstrations by groups of concerned citizens, often armed with our research and campaign material.

We didn't slow down for a moment. Only two days after

Ambassador Dean's visit, Mel Hurtig appeared before the Commons
Foreign Affairs Committee after having just completed his fourteen-city
book tour promoting his new book, *Rushing to Armageddon*. He held up
one newspaper clipping after another and told the all-party committee
members,

> There's so much here. Look: "Pentagon ready to weaponize
> space"; "U.S. military lays out plan to wage war in space";
> "U.S. ready to put weapons in space." There's absolutely no
> doubt about this. Do you really want to live in a world where
> you go out of your home, look up, and see orbiting weapons
> circling the world, knowing full well that the Russians and the
> Chinese are going to respond to this?

The constant repetition of our message was having an effect. I once
spent some time with U.S. consumer activist Ralph Nader during his visit
to Ottawa, and during our discussions he said, "Those who underestimate
the power of repetition don't understand how a jackhammer works."

The media, perhaps finally sensing that missile defence indeed
might not be a done deal, began to entertain the thought that Paul
Martin might actually say no. In fact, I distinctly recall the first moment
when I heard a reporter imply such an outcome. I was taking questions
at a press conference when CBC-TV news reporter Julie van Dusen
posed a question to us that was based on the premise that Paul Martin
might not join missile defence. Clearly this idea was making its way
through the National Press Gallery at this point. In fact, the *Toronto Star*
summed it up by saying, "More and more, it is the missile defence
opponents who are getting their message out."

* * *

To this day, no one has satisfactorily explained what Canadian participation in missile defence would entail. Exactly what would be
Canada's role in the program?

Unlike the establishment of NORAD decades ago, which required
Canadian territory to erect radar stations, the Bush administration's

missile-defence system did not require the use of Canadian territory. Without radars, it was unlikely there would be a need for missile interceptors to be located in Canada.

Would Canadian equipment be needed? Today all of NORAD's missile-detection–and-tracking equipment is owned by the United States. Canada's contribution to NORAD comes in the form of radar sites for air defence, not missile-launch warning and tracking.

What about funding or Canadian technology? The United States spends nearly ten billion dollars a year on missile defence, which is roughly the equivalent of the entire Canadian military budget. Even a billion dollars a year from Canada would make only a small contribution to the program's budget.

And if Canadian technology were needed, the Pentagon is always free to enter contracts with Canadian companies without Canadian government approval. Nonetheless, only a single missile-defence contract—with CAE Inc. of Montreal and worth an unknown amount— was ever disclosed.

In fact, according to the CAE's former CEO Derek H. Burney, when Canada announced it was not participating in BMD, the contract was cancelled. This would indicate that it was politically motivated in the first place in order to get the company's influential CEO to lobby the government for missile defence.

So, if Canadian territory, funding, or technology was not required by the Americans, just who was requesting Canadian participation from whom? Was the U.S. urging Canada to come inside the missile-defence program, or was Canada banging at the door asking to be let in? The answer is unclear.

In December 2004, the *Ottawa Citizen* published the contents of a previously secret Department of National Defence report, which the newspaper had received under the Access to Information Act. It explored how Canada could contribute to the shield. The DND report had been produced in May 2002 for the government.

The report included a list of ways that Canada could contribute to the U.S. missile shield, including providing a missile-tracking site in the North or on the East Coast, providing funding or helping to design weapons for the system, and even providing political support for the program. While the initial system, intended to defend against missile attacks from North Korea or China, had radar tracking systems in Alaska to cover the West Coast, a site on Canada's East Coast would assist in providing coverage against missile attacks from the Middle East as the system developed.

A battery of missile interceptors would likely accompany a radar site, since the system works best when it has radars and intercepts located close together. An earlier DND report from May 2001 noted that the installation of tracking systems on Canada's East Coast would allow Canada to provide a "value-added role" in the shield and faster warning of a missile launch from the Middle East.

Contributing to the mystery surrounding the nature of the ongoing Canada–U.S. discussion on missile defence were the comments by an unidentified U.S. State Department official reported in the *Toronto Star* on September 28, 2004. "It depends on what Canada wants," the official said, adding that Canada may have to contribute military personnel, cash, and even land if it wanted Canadian cities to be protected under the defence umbrella. These comments underscored the fact that the system did not require Canadian participation for the U.S. to move ahead with its own shield, though the use of NORAD made it more convenient for them. The only issue apparently remaining was whether the Canadian government wished Canada's territory to be included in the shield's protective cover.

The official said that, under the missile shield's configuration at the time, protection of Canada would only be incidental. "Let me emphasize, incidental capability to defend North America and Canadian territory," he told the *Star*. "I can't tell you 50 percent, 60 percent or 10 percent of Canada would be protected by the limited system."

To protect some, or all, of Canada, more missiles than the sixteen planned for the continental system would be required. "[Sixteen] is not going to protect 100 percent of Canadian territory," the official said:

> If the Canadian government wants to participate in terms of defending North America and in particular Canadian territory,

there would have to be subsequent negotiations that involve technical aspects, financial aspects, things like in-kind contributions, maybe Canadian military personnel, maybe even territory.

It's a Canadian decision how they want to participate in the program. If Canada wants its own dedicated [missile] interceptors, that's something to be decided.

These comments by the unnamed U.S. State Department official provide a great deal of clarity to the murky issue of Canada's role in the program, and it boils down to this: The United States does not need Canada for this missile-defence system.

Even the NORAD amendment, while welcomed as a convenience by the United States, was not required, since all of the missile-monitoring satellites and radars used by NORAD are owned by the United States and it could easily move that function to another U.S. command.

So one can assume that the United States was not pressuring Canada to join to make its shield operate. If there was any pressure, it was merely to gain Canada's political endorsement of the controversial system.

However, if Canada wanted to provide protection all the way from Windsor to Iqaluit, this would be a technical issue requiring a reconfiguring of the current system, which is designed to defend only the United States. As a Canadian foreign-affairs official told parliamentarians during a special briefing, "For Canada there are a number of critical considerations. First is protection. The primary goal of any Canadian engagement [in BMD] would have to enhance the security of Canada and Canadians. Canada may receive some degree of protection from the system even if we do not cooperate. But if we are not cooperating, we would not be able to rely on the U.S. to provide such protection."

And here one can see the absolutely delusional nature of these absurd negotiations, for what Canadian actually believed there was any threat whatsoever of a missile attack against Canada? Could the Department of National Defence produce even a single study that demonstrated that Canada required protection against missile attacks?

Even the most ardent supporters of missile defence rarely, if ever, said that Canada needed protection. They always focused on satisfying the needs of the United States so that it could go ahead with its program, or at least ensuring that NORAD continued. But defending Canada?

So, if it is true that the United States was seeking only Canada's political endorsement, and possibly the eventual use of the East Coast for a redundant radar installation many years in the future as the shield developed, then how could Paul Martin put a deal before parliament that committed even a million dollars or an hectare of territory for this defence system—a system that even Canada's top generals could not honestly argue was needed for Canada's defence?

The fact is, he couldn't. So he began to set out markers, or conditions, for Canadian participation in the program. Anyone listening closely could hear the beginning of the climb-down from missile defence during the prime minister's annual year-end interviews.

On Tuesday night, December 14, 2004, I sat watching the CBC-TV news, as host Peter Mansbridge raised the issue of missile defence in his fireside chat with Paul Martin. He asked, "Why is it so hard for us to make up our mind on this? Either you're for it or not."

The prime minister replied,

> We had to make up our minds on the provision of information in order to protect NORAD and we did it within two weeks of the election, right away ... Now you go to the next stage. We made it very clear, number one, we're not going to have the weaponization of space. Number two, our defence priorities in terms of North America, our coasts, our common frontier with the United States, and our sovereignty in the Arctic. That's where our priorities lie.... I [am] not yet satisfied as to the nature of the voice that Canada will have in it, nor am I yet satisfied as to the nature and evolution of [its] development. When I have the answers to those questions, then we will make the decision.

The prime minister added, "We understand the importance to them, and we do not object to the Americans defending themselves, but as far as we're concerned, we have certain questions, and until they're answered, we are not going to make that decision."

In other interviews, the prime minister reiterated his demands: that there be no additional cost to Canada, that there be no use of Canadian territory for missiles, that Canada have demonstrable influence and insight into the development of the system, and that space weapons not be involved.

With these conditions, it was becoming virtually impossible for Paul Martin to deliver an agreement to parliament for a promised debate and vote that was also supported by the United States. For instance, how could the government demonstrate that it had influence over the system if it was controlled by the U.S.-only Northern Command (as determined by the Americans), rather than the joint Canada–U.S. NORAD command?

Our campaign had clearly advanced from achieving a delay in the Canadian decision to forcing the government to put limits on Canadian participation, and was coming very close to achieving our third and best-case scenario, which was Paul Martin saying "no" to missile defence.

But while the Canadian news media and some in his own caucus were complaining about the government's delays, the United States government was announcing a delay of its own. The missile-defence system would *not* be declared operational before the end of 2004, as President Bush had pledged.

This announcement by the Pentagon came only a few days after a test of the system failed, the first test in two years. A target missile was launched from Kodiac Island in Alaska, but the new missile interceptor didn't launch from the Ronald Reagan Ballistic Missile Defense Test Site in Kwajalein Atoll in the South Pacific. The Pentagon said the eighty-five–million-dollar test failed because of an "unknown anomaly." The target missile dropped into the sea.

* * *

Throughout January 2005, the fallout from President Bush's visit continued to rain down on Paul Martin's head. The details of the strong words President Bush used with Martin behind closed doors began to leak out. Had President Bush been strong-arming Martin to join missile defence, or was he just restating what he had been saying all along? The spin doctors were working overtime to control the damage.

U.S. Ambassador Paul Cellucci, weighing in on the issue once again, said he hoped Canada would join missile defence, but tried to soften the message by adding that there was no hurry. Bill Graham replied through the media, "We're going to do it in light of our own democratic process, and we'll make the right decision in the fullness of time."

The issue followed the Liberal caucus as they travelled to a retreat in my hometown of Fredericton, New Brunswick. Graham was on the defensive, arguing that he did not feel pressure to join missile defence from the Americans. "The Americans have made it very clear, Ambassador Cellucci and others, that they would prefer that Canada join the missile-defence system," he acknowledged, despite saying he felt no pressure.

Despite the sub-freezing temperatures, a handful of demonstrators stood outside the hotel where the Liberals were meeting, handing out anti-missile-defence leaflets produced by the Polaris Institute. Bill Graham threw on a coat and came out to talk to the demonstrators; he told them he was listening to their concerns. It was another encouraging sign.

But the campaign was becoming overstretched financially. The Ploughshares Fund, a foundation in California, came through with enough funding to keep the campaign afloat.

With the government sending out positive signals, we looked for every opportunity to keep up the pressure. Early in the new year, an unexpected development presented us with another such opportunity.

The government needed to fill the office of Canadian ambassador to the United States, with the departure of the previous ambassador, Michel Kergin. Former New Brunswick premier Frank McKenna was rumoured to be the leading candidate for the job. McKenna had spent the years following his retirement from politics making a fortune from his law practice and accepting many high-powered corporate board appointments, including those with the Bank of Montreal and General Motors of Canada.

One part of his résumé touted by his backers was his membership on the Canadian Advisory Board of the Carlyle Group, a little-known, but very wealthy, private investment firm headquartered in Washington, D.C. The Carlyle Group controlled more than eighteen billion dollars in investments in companies that profited from government connections, particularly companies in the defence, aerospace, and telecommunications industry.

The Carlyle Group was dubbed "the ex-presidents' club" by the *Guardian* newspaper because of the firm's success in recruiting an array of former politicians to senior management and directorships. Its membership has included John Major, a former British prime minister; James A. Baker III, George Bush, Sr.'s former secretary of state; and Frank Carlucci, Ronald Reagan's former defense secretary and a former deputy director of the CIA. Former president George Bush, Sr., had served on its Asia advisory board from 1998 until 2003, and Fidel Ramos, former president of the Philippines, served on the Asia advisory board until 2004.

I had written an opinion piece for the *Toronto Star* back in 2002 on McKenna's connections to the Carlyle Group, along with those of other Canadian corporate titans. McKenna had organized meetings of Canadian CEOs for the Carlyle Group in Canada, and reportedly became quite good friends with George Bush, Sr. His rumoured appointment as U.S. ambassador spurred some people to start tossing the old article back and forth across the Internet on various e-mail lists and Web sites.

Reviewing the research for that article, I began to wonder what impact McKenna's appointment would have on the missile-defence debate. Given his close connections to the Bush family and this powerful U.S.-based fund, how would Frank McKenna represent all of Canada to the United States—and not just the wealthiest Canadians? Did his financial dealings suggest there might be a conflict of interest if, as was expected, he intended to help shape Canadian government policy?

I talked it over with Tony Clarke, and we decided to put together a brief that articulated these questions. In addition, given these concerns, we would make the case that Frank McKenna's appointment should be reviewed by the all-party Commons Foreign Affairs Committee. In fact, during the Liberal leadership race, Paul Martin had said that major government appointments should be reviewed by parliament. How could he refuse, given that the position of Canadian ambassador to the United States was one of the most important appointments made by the government?

So I set to work preparing what became an eight-page brief that Tony dubbed "The McKenna File." We released it at a well-attended press conference on Parliament Hill on January 11, 2005. Soon Frank McKenna's connection to the Carlyle Group, which had once been touted as a benefit to him, became the subject of a lot of questions, especially in relation to his views on continental defence, the arms industry, and missile defence.

After we released the report, CTV reporter Rosemary Thompson asked me to come up to their television studios to record a brief interview. By sheer coincidence, both my taping and a taping of an interview with Frank McKenna on another CTV program were scheduled for the same time.

As I stood just inside the front door to the CTV studios being interviewed by Rosemary with cameras rolling, Frank McKenna walked through the door. At that exact moment I was saying the line that was used that night on the news: "Will Frank McKenna look at all of the issues involving issues like missile defence, or will he just say, 'Good for the bottom line. Let's go with it'?"

Whether he heard me or not I don't know, but later in the "green room," he was having his make-up done and was engrossed in a discussion with another CTV journalist, Craig Oliver. I thought for a moment that perhaps I should introduce myself, and had he been there alone or if we had made eye contact, I might have. Instead, I just let myself out of the room.

That day, reporters essentially read directly from my report, and posed my rhetorical questions to McKenna practically verbatim in a fast-paced media scrum when they caught him outside the prime minister's office: "Why didn't you tell the Prime Minister about your extraneous role or your current role [with the] Carlyle Group in Washington? Did you tell him you were going to sever that tie? How about your links with the companies selling armaments? What is your personal view of missile defence and whether Canada should get involved in missile defence?"

Frank McKenna tried to downplay his connections to the Carlyle Group and the Bush family: "I think that my connections ... have probably been overblown," he said. "I would have some relationships, but am I cozy with folks? I'm afraid I'm not. But I do have enough relationships to form the basis of a good working relationship."

Tony and I were surprised ourselves at how we turned what looked like a certainty for McKenna's appointment into an issue involving corporate interest, connection with the Bush family and other Washington hawks, and missile defence. We were clear that we weren't opposing his appointment, but, as I wrote in the report, "McKenna's previous business and political associations are enough to raise serious questions about his suitability for the role of Canadian Ambassador to the United States."

But most importantly, our central recommendation in the McKenna File—that he appear before the Commons Foreign Affairs Committee—was agreed to by all the political parties. So, sometime in the coming weeks between his appointment and taking office, Frank McKenna would appear before the all-party committee of MPs to answer questions about missile defence and many other issues.

What we didn't know is that we had just set in motion a series of events that would usher in the conclusion of missile defence, round one.

* * *

February 2005 arrived, and with it a failed missile-defence test, another plea to the government from U.S. Ambassador Cellucci and the defence lobby to join missile defence, and yet another poll showing a growing majority opposed to it. Time was running out for missile defence.

On February 14, the Missile Defence Agency tried to repeat the eighty-five-million-dollar missile test that had failed only a few months earlier. The test "enemy" missile launched as expected from Alaska, but the new missile interceptor once again refused to launch from the Reagan Test Site. The test missile again dropped harmlessly into the ocean.

Prior to the last test in December, the first in two years, the system had gone five for eight in highly scripted intercept tests. It was now five for ten.

The public was becoming accustomed to reports of missile-defence malfunctions and missed deadlines. Likewise, CEOs and military leaders exhorting Canada to join missile defence were about as routine as the test failures. And their arguments were just as ineffective.

In New York, another conference of government officials, academics, diplomats, and others on Canada–U.S. relations concluded that—surprise, surprise—Canada should join missile defence. While the conference was held in the United States, the majority of participants were reportedly Canadian.

"Even though Canada does not share the U.S. assessment of external threats to the same degree, it has no alternative but to adjust to U.S. perceptions of what menaces North America," said a discussion paper prepared by the American Assembly at Columbia University.

Pamela Wallin, who had obviously lost touch with the Canadian public during her tenure as Canada's consul general to New York, said she believed most Canadians supported signing on, despite successive polls showing otherwise.

Back in Canada, the Conference of Defence Associations, a pro-military lobby group headed by retired military brass, issued a statement of their own arguing that "If Canada sits on the sidelines, it is clear that it will not have a voice or any influence over the future direction of the program." Sensing that momentum was slipping away, the group said, "The CDA believes the Prime Minister needs to explain to his caucus, to other political parties and to the people of Canada that there is a mutual interest in co-operating with the U.S. on defence and security issues such as missile defence."

A few days later U.S. ambassador Paul Cellucci repeated his by-now-familiar refrain and told a Calgary audience, "We believe it's in Canada's sovereign interest to be part of the decision-making process."

But the arguments were becoming thinner and thinner. NORAD's future was secure, so what arguments were left? Essentially, no one believed there was a missile threat to Canada, they were indifferent to missile-defence contracts for Canadian companies, they were becoming convinced that the system did not work, and most importantly, they were suspicious of Bush's intentions—especially about space weapons.

What greater evidence of the cooling on missile defence could there have been than the sight of the government's chief proponent of joining, Defence Minister Bill Graham, arguing that missile defence was not a dead issue? Canadian Press suggested, "Canadian participation—which seemed highly likely as recently as last fall—is now a dead duck." In response, Graham reminded the reporter that "the decision has not been taken yet."

A new EKOS poll was released in mid-February that must have sent a chill through the prime minister's office. Opposition to missile defence stood at 54 percent nationally and was creeping upward. Meanwhile, support for the system had dropped, with only 34 percent saying they supported or strongly supported joining, down from 37 percent in October 2004.

EKOS president, Frank Graves, told the *Toronto Star* that "For Mr. Martin and the Liberals it's evolved from being a relatively benign issue to one that could be genuinely troubling." Public support had plunged twenty percentage points in the last few years, an indicator of "deep anxieties about what the American Administration [is] doing," added Graves.

But what was most telling about the poll was the importance people were attaching to the issue. "Moreover, people tell us that unlike issues like same-sex [marriage] or ethics, this is an issue which may be worth fighting an election over."

In a minority government, Paul Martin could not control when the government would fall and an election would have to be called. Jack Layton had said he was willing to work with the government to keep parliament functioning, but he drew the line at missile defence. He would treat this issue as one of confidence in the government. If the government lost a vote of confidence, it would have to call an election, handing the missile defence issue to Jack Layton and Gilles Duceppe.

When our campaign had begun in early 2004, we wanted to make missile defence an issue in the upcoming election in June 2004. We had had some success that year, but it now appeared that we had paved the way to make the next election—in 2005—the election about missile defence. It seemed that no election since the 1988 "free trade" election could become so defined by a single issue, and missile defence would be the "ballot question" on the public's mind.

Every political party was trying to get into the right position on the issue, including the Conservatives. But it was a game of musical chairs, and the Liberals risked being the party left standing when the music stopped.

* * *

Sara and I targeted the Liberal Party convention as our next opportunity to push the issue. We had to help ensure that the motion against missile defence passed with a strong majority. While no policy vote by the party would bind the government, a motion against missile defence would be a public humiliation for Martin. We had to make sure that, like a ball and chain attached to his ankle, Martin could not shake the problems associated with this issue.

The convention was planned for March 3 to 5 at the Ottawa Congress Centre. Political conventions, especially Liberal ones, were unknown territory for me. Somewhere between all the receptions and parties, delegates from across Canada would vote on policy issues. The weekend would culminate in a vote of confidence in their party leader, which organizers wanted to pass with a near-unanimous verdict.

It was obvious that we couldn't do anything as elaborate as organizing delegates on the convention floor for the missile-defence vote, but maybe we could help others who could. So Sara set about trying to make contact with the Young Liberals to find someone we could work with. Later, Sara came into my office and said, "I just got off the phone with Denise Brunson, the national director of the Young Liberals. She's totally on side with us on missile defence."

Two days later Sara, Denise, and I met in my office. Over the next hour we talked about missile defence, and Denise filled us in on what had been happening inside the party.

First, she explained that a motion from the B.C. Young Liberals against missile defence would automatically go to the convention floor for a vote. The Young Liberals out West were coming under a lot of pressure from people in the party establishment, particularly in the prime minister's office, to withdraw the resolution. But Denise said their resolve was strong and they had the support of the Women's Caucus and the Quebec Caucus. Both had passed anti-missile-defence resolutions of their own, but they were going to consolidate their efforts behind the Young Liberals' motion.

We offered to help write and provide an expert review of some of their materials so that their arguments would be bulletproof. We also discussed bringing in a high-profile person to meet with delegates, and possibly hosting a hospitality suite.

We did not have a clear idea of who our "ringer" would be for the Liberal convention, until I went up to Parliament Hill to discuss convention strategy with Lynn Myers, our friend and Liberal MP from Kitchener–Conestoga. I was invited to go into his office, where Lynn was on the phone, just finishing a conversation. When he hung up he said, "That was Mel Hurtig calling to talk about missile defence."

Then it dawned on me: Mel Hurtig could be just the person to connect with progressive, nationalistic Liberals. Lynn and I talked about inviting him, and he agreed that Mel would make a strong impact. Moreover, Lynn offered to join us in hosting Mel and organizing the hospitality suite.

Lynn had more encouraging news. He explained that the Young Liberals held a lot of influence within the party, because they were strong supporters of Paul Martin's leadership bid. Further, he told us it was not just the Young Liberals, the Women's Caucus, and the Quebec

Caucus that had submitted anti-missile-defence resolutions, but that many riding associations had passed resolutions of their own. There were at least twenty resolutions coming up from the grassroots of the Liberal Party. Any controversy over same-sex marriage paled in comparison to missile defence.

Our plan was coming together for the Liberal convention. We had a suite booked, Mel Hurtig had agreed to come to the convention, and we were preparing some leaflets to promote Mel's availability at our "Star Wars hospitality suite."

Then we learned that the missile-defence lobby had laid plans too. The Conference of Defence Associations had organized their own missile defence event, only it was going to be held in the Fairmont Château Laurier Hotel, right across the street from the Liberal convention. Ambassador Paul Cellucci was scheduled to be their speaker.

It was coming down to a head-to-head match between the Conference of Defence Associations and the Polaris Institute, Paul Cellucci versus Mel Hurtig. I thought this was likely going to be the last, great showdown on missile defence. Too bad it never happened.

* * *

On Tuesday, February 22, 2005, I was scheduled to appear before the Commons Foreign Affairs Committee to make a presentation not directly related to missile defence, but on proposed legislation regarding Canada's satellite program. I was to be joined by my colleague from Duke University, Michael Byers, who had relocated to the University of British Columbia, and by Ross Neil, who also hailed from UBC.

But there was another reason for me to trek up to the committee room on Parliament Hill that morning: the witness appearing before the committee just before me was the soon-to-be Canadian ambassador to the United States, Frank McKenna.

As we had recommended in our report, "The McKenna File," in January, Frank McKenna was going to have his day before the all-party committee in a friendly discussion, to answer questions and discuss his new job. The room was filled to capacity. Michael, Ross, Wade Huntley, another visiting colleague from UBC, and I sat together, pressed up against the side wall of the conference room, listening to the MPs posing their questions to McKenna.

It was clear that every member of that committee had read "The McKenna File". Many of them had lifted their questions and evidence right from the pages I had written—not just members from the NDP but the Conservatives as well. I was waiting for the first question about missile defence.

I didn't have to wait long. Conservative member Kevin Sorensen, asking the first question following McKenna's opening remarks, asked, "Have you discussed continental defence, and in particular the ballistic missile defence system, with the prime minister of our country or with any members of his Cabinet?" McKenna avoided answering the question directly.

NDP leader Jack Layton, who didn't normally attend the committee, asked, "Is there nothing about the missile-defence plan that you would find troubling?" McKenna gave an honest answer: "Quite honestly, I have not been able to discover what it is the Americans actually want from us with respect to missile defence." No doubt he was as perplexed as anyone who had examined the issue closely.

After about another hour of questions, the hearing ended, and reporters and cameras crowded into the room. I stepped out into the hallway to talk to reporters, and I did not realize that McKenna was also being interviewed in a media scrum just inside the doorway.

Following the break the meeting resumed and Michael, Ross, and I took our places at the hearing table, where McKenna had just been seated; we continued for another few hours discussing satellites. Meanwhile a storm was brewing in newsrooms across the city.

After the hearing Ross, Wade, and I decided to have lunch at the Parliamentary Pub restaurant. We were just finishing when my cell phone rang. I was very surprised to hear the voice of Aaron Gairdner, the Conservative Party's defence researcher whom I had first met at Gordon O'Connor's office. "Did you hear about McKenna?" he asked.

"What do you mean? I just came from there," I replied.

"He said that Canada is already in missile defence. It's all over the news," Aaron told me.

I filled in my colleagues and then headed back to the office to see what was happening. As I made my way down Metcalfe Street to the Polaris Institute's office on Cooper Street, one thought kept going through my mind: "This is our moment. We have to push the government to make a decision now."

When I got to the office, Sara and I scanned news Web sites. Apparently, while I had been outside the room, reporters had asked McKenna about missile defence in the scrum. He said, "We are part of it now, and the question is what more do we need?" No wonder his comments were going out on all the news stations. He had just contradicted the government's central argument: that we were not part of the system because no decision had been made.

McKenna, of course, was referring to the change to NORAD the previous summer, which allowed missile-tracking data to be shared with the U.S. command that runs the shield. "There's no doubt, in looking back, that the NORAD amendment has given, has created part—in fact a great deal—of what the United States means in terms of being able to get the input for defensive weaponry," he said.

But at the time the NORAD amendment was announced, Bill Graham had said that the change in no way meant that Canada was joining the system. It was August 5, 2004, and I had been there myself in the foyer of the House of Commons with Graham. "This decision does not affect or in any way determine the ultimate decision as to whether Canada will participate in missile defence," he told reporters.

Ottawa was buzzing with speculation about McKenna's comments. Was this part of some strategy to roll out a decision to join? A decision not to join? Or did McKenna just make a mistake?

I received a call from Mike Duffy, the *CTV News* political reporter. "What's your take on this, Steve?" he asked.

"I think he screwed up, Mike," I said. "What he said is essentially true. If the Americans wanted anything from us, it was to use NORAD's missile-tracking abilities rather than having to go through the inconvenience of creating a system of their own. Beyond that it's not clear what else they want from us."

Duffy told me he had heard from a CTV cameraman who bumped

into McKenna as he was walking down the road from the Parliament Buildings after the hearing, and McKenna was whistling away as if he hadn't a care in the world.

That would support my conclusion that he made a mistake and was unaware of its impact. What he said was really a message intended for him to deliver to an American audience once he was on the job in Washington. If Americans asked him when Canada was going to join, he could reply that Canada was essentially in. McKenna's mistake was that he delivered the message in Canada.

The result of McKenna's comment was to further muddy the waters on whether or not Canada was "part of" missile defence. The NORAD amendment had come to be viewed in two ways: a clever means for Canada to "join" missile defence and satisfy the Americans without angering the public, or simply a technical change that firmly ensconced the operation and control of the missile-defence system inside a U.S.-only command—not NORAD—thereby keeping Canada outside of the system but letting the Americans get on with building their own system.

The truth is that the only people who held the view that Canada had cleverly "joined" missile defence with the NORAD amendment in the summer of 2004 were missile-defence opponents. But what they missed was the fact that not a single missile-defence proponent, including George W. Bush himself, seemed to be satisfied by the NORAD amendment. In fact, calls to join the U.S. system only intensified in the fall of 2004.

But McKenna's misstep gave the opposition parties plenty of ammunition to demand that the government come clean with its position. It was now impossible for Paul Martin to delay any further. They didn't need any prompting, but I made a few calls and sent a few e-mails anyway just to voice my encouragement that our friends on the Hill press as hard as possible.

Bill Graham tried to recover during the raucous Question Period in Parliament that day, as opposition parties hammered the government. Graham repeated that Canada had agreed to the NORAD amendment, but the government had not yet made any decisions in terms of ballistic-missile defence.

We weighed in with our own press release that afternoon with the headline, "Gov't Risks Election Over McKenna Remark on Missile Defence":

Frank McKenna's statement that Canada is already "part of" the U.S. missile defence system leaves the Opposition parties positioned to force a decision from Paul Martin—if not an election.

It is doubtful that Opposition parties will accept a "we are still studying the issue" response from the Prime Minister, nor merely a retraction from Frank McKenna.

They could press the Prime Minister to finally make a decision on Canada's participation in missile defence. If the Prime Minister backs his Canadian Ambassador to the U.S. (designate) that Canada has joined, then this would violate the amendment to the Throne Speech which committed the government to a vote in Parliament before a final decision is made, setting the stage for a non-confidence motion.

A recent EKOS poll (Feb. 14, 2005) found that 57 percent of Canadians said yes/maybe to the questions of whether Canada's participation in missile defence was important enough to force an election over (by comparison, only 38 per ent felt the same about same-sex marriage.)

We got the answer we were looking for very quickly. That evening, February 22, 2005, at 9:50 p.m., Canadian Press reported that the government would deliver a firm "no" on Canadian participation in the U.S. missile-defence system. They were quoting a report from Radio-Canada, the French-language CBC network, that had broken the story only moments earlier. According to the Canadian Press report, Prime Minister Martin would make the announcement on Thursday, February 24.

I got a call at home from Sara. "Have you seen the news. We've won!" she said. We were both elated, but it was hard to shake the feeling that maybe this was a trick. We had become suspicious of the government's strategy.

The next morning, I began my Wednesday very early with an interview on CTV's *Canada AM* to discuss the unfolding drama of missile defence. As I walked to downtown Ottawa from my home near the Rideau Canal in the pre-dawn light, I could see that all the newspaper boxes were brimming with newspapers carrying banner headlines: "PM set to reject missile defence: After McKenna Says Canada Is In, Martin Will Announce that It's Out," read the *Globe and Mail's* headline. "PM Rejects Missile Plan: Martin to Make Position Clear after Day of Confusion," said the *Toronto Star*. "PM to Say 'No' to Missile Shield: McKenna's Musings that We'd Already Joined U.S. Defence Program Force Martin's Hand," said the *Ottawa Citizen*. "Missile Snub: After Months of Sitting on Defence, PM to Deliver Firm 'No' to U.S. Plan," read the *Ottawa Sun*. "Le Missile McKenna," quipped *Le Devoir*, and "Le Canada participe déjà au bouclier antimissile," said *La Presse*.

I arrived at the TV studio and was seated, once again, in a little room with an earphone in my ear, a microphone clipped to my lapel, staring down the lens of a TV camera. The other guest was long-time missile proponent, and a person I had debated several years ago on CBC's *CounterSpin*, Professor James Fergusson of the University of Manitoba. He was in a studio in Winnipeg. Our host, Jane Taber, was in Toronto.

"Mr. Staples, you must be pretty happy today," Jane said. I replied that yes, it looked like we had come to the end of this chapter in the missile-defence story; Paul Martin was set to say "no" to missile defence.

But Jim Fergusson was still holding out hope. "I think [Paul Martin] may just simply say that no decision has been made, which has been government policy for quite a while," he said.

I replied that Martin had nowhere else to go, with unreliable support from the Conservatives and problems in his own party. "He's got a divided caucus. There's a Liberal convention coming up. The grassroots of the party is sending at least twenty resolutions up through the queue against missile defence." I pointed out the recent EKOS poll that found that 57 percent of Canadians felt missile defence was important enough to go to an election. "I think that was the last nail in the coffin," I said.

I spent the rest of the day spreading the good news that our campaign had been a success. Sara and I called and e-mailed people all over Canada to thank them for their help and to encourage them to celebrate the victory that they had worked so hard to attain. I contacted General Gard and Jonathan Dean in the United States and Alan Simpson in the U.K. I spoke with Mel Hurtig and told him that he could spend those days we had planned for him to be in Ottawa for the Liberal convention relaxing at home in Edmonton instead.

Peter Coombes and I plastered a giant banner across Ceasefire.ca that declared, "We win!" And we sent a letter to our thousands of supporters who had joined the campaign through the Web site.

The widely expected final decision was not announced on Wednesday, because this was the day for the government to bring out its annual budget—a very elaborate affair involving a major budget speech from the finance minister and reams of financial documents.

The final announcement was made by the government on Thursday, February 24, 2005. The first public announcement was not by Prime Minister Martin, but came in a speech to the House of Commons by Foreign Affairs Minister Pierre Pettigrew. After outlining the billions of dollars the government was committing to defence and security in the budget, Pettigrew said this:

> The Government has been studying the question of ballistic missile defence for some time. We have been in close contact with our counterparts in the United States. The U.S. has weighed the anticipated danger to its citizens and territory against available resources, and has decided to proceed with deployment of a missile defence system. This is their right, and we understand and respect their decision.
>
> Canada, however, must act in its own interests, and must determine where its own priorities lie. We must determine

where investments will bring the greatest tangible results. After careful consideration of the issue of missile defence, we will not participate in the U.S. ballistic missile defence system.

That morning, Peggy Mason and I were on a train headed to a conference in Montreal on promoting peace in space, where we were to meet with others, including Sarah Estabrooks and Ernie Regehr from Project Ploughshares, and Theresa Hitchens from the U.S.-based Center for Defense Information. When we arrived in Montreal, Sara Kemp told me over the phone that Pettigrew had delivered his speech and that Martin was scheduled to make his own announcement later in the day.

As we shared the news and congratulations, we decided we should arrange a "champagne popping" ceremony and invite the television stations to come and join us at our meeting at McGill University. I called some newsrooms and Peggy and I found a liquor store and bought a bottle of cheap champagne and some plastic cups.

Meanwhile in Ottawa, Paul Martin, looking rather dour, stood uncomfortably in front of a temporary podium erected just outside his office door and told reporters:

We had an extensive discussion led by the Ministers of Foreign Affairs and National Defence, concerning the invitation to participate in the evolution of the proposed ballistic missile defence system.

It is in respect of that discussion that we are announcing today that Canada will not take part in the proposed ballistic missile defence system.

Let me be clear: we respect the right of the United States to defend itself and its people. Indeed, we will continue to work in partnership with our southern neighbours on the common defence of North America and on continental security.

However, ballistic missile defence is not where we will concentrate our efforts. Instead we will act—both alone and with our neighbours—on defence priorities such as those outlined in yesterday's budget. These include: strengthening the security of our common border, bolstering security at points of entry, reinforcing our coastal and arctic sovereignty, increasing support for intelligence, expanding our armed forces and increasing our capital investment in helicopters, trucks, aircrafts and ships.

As part of this, Canada remains steadfast in its support of NORAD, which is essential to continental security and our national sovereignty. That's why we agreed last summer to enhance our longstanding commitment to track missiles through NORAD. We stand by that commitment. It underscores an important ongoing partnership with the United States and most of all, it is in Canada's strategic national interest.

Canada will also continue to work closely with the United States—and with other allies—on security and defence matters right around the world. The examples of mutual interest are many—we are partners in combating global terrorism, in Afghanistan and Haiti we have worked side by side to promote stability and security. In the Middle East, Canada intends to play an enhanced role. For Iraq we will provide training and are contributing to the NATO fund. We are also collaborating on efforts to stop the proliferation of nuclear weapons to powers such as Iran. In numerous failed and failing states we are helping to keep the peace and build institutions of good government.

Canada recognizes the enormous burden that the United States shoulders when it comes to international peace and security. The substantial increases made yesterday to our defence budget are a tangible indication that Canada intends to carry its full share of that global responsibility. In the foreign and defence papers to be released soon we will elaborate further on how we will discharge these international responsibilities.

In concluding, let me say that Canada and the United States remain one another's staunchest allies and closest friends. Our respect for, and our commitment to one another, and to the ideals we share as nations, is unwavering. Our mutual commitment to a safer and more secure world is resolute. Finally, we will continue to ensure that our overall relationship grows stronger and that our people enjoy increased security and prosperity in the years ahead.

After taking a few questions, Paul Martin turned and walked back into his office and shut the door.

The cameras came to meet us at McGill University, and we gathered around a newspaper with the headline "PM Rejects Missile Plan," uncorked the bottle of champagne with a pop, filled our glasses, and made a toast to our success. It was the sweetest champagne I had ever tasted. That night the stations broadcast the news of the announcement and CTV carried footage of our little celebration for such a large victory across the country.

* * *

In the days after the decision, reporters pieced together when the decision had been made and how it had been communicated to the United States and, of course, the public. The final days before the announcement were not unlike the government's handling of the issue itself: delayed, disorganized, and rather deceptive.

According to reports, the prime minister made the decision to not join the U.S. missile-defence system the week before it was announced. The decision was tied to the unveiling of the federal budget on Wednesday, February 23. In essence, the prime minister intended to pump billions into the defence budget to buy his way out of missile defence, so that he could announce his "no" decision without looking as though he was weak on the defence and military issues.

According to the *Globe and Mail*, Prime Minister Martin and Finance Minister Ralph Goodale met on February 11 to determine the size of the defence spending increase in the budget. They decided it would be substantial, and on budget day the increase was $12.8 billion over five years—the largest increase in a generation, and one that would send military spending well above Cold War levels and higher than any level since the Second World War.

Then, on Thursday, February 17, a full week before the day the decision was to be announced publicly, Martin met with his most senior ministers to discuss missile defence. According to the *Globe and Mail*, the prime minister was worried that the issue was dividing the Liberal caucus and the country and threatening to cause him great embarrassment at the Liberal convention, where a motion to not join was expected to pass by a wide margin.

"The Prime Minister told officials that he would make a decision on this over the course of the weekend." According to one source who spoke to the *Globe*, "He wanted the week to unfold in a way that we would be advising the Americans at NATO that the budget would demonstrate our bona fides with respect to defence and that we would make a public announcement on BMD shortly thereafter." The prime minister was "leaning" towards "no."

Prime Minister Martin and Foreign Affairs Minister Pettigrew then travelled to Brussels for a NATO summit held February 20 to 22, 2005. According to the *Globe*, it was while aboard the government jet en route to Brussels that Paul Martin told his advisers that Canada would not be participating in the U.S. missile-defence system. He added that he would soften the blow by making the announcement one day after making a large increase in defence spending in the budget.

Despite having the opportunity at the NATO summit, Paul Martin did not personally inform President Bush, who also attended the summit. Instead, he left it to Pettigrew to tell the Americans.

On the last day of the NATO summit, Tuesday, February 22—the same day Frank McKenna appeared before the Commons Foreign Affairs Committee—Foreign Affairs Minister Pierre Pettigrew informed U.S. Secretary of State Condoleezza Rice of Canada's decision to not participate in BMD. The news was also conveyed through diplomats in Ottawa and Washington.

U.S. ambassador-designate Frank McKenna apparently was not informed that a decision had been made, even though Pettigrew spoke to Rice that very day. According to some reports, McKenna "went ballistic" over the news that he had been left out of the loop.

Later, Defence Minister Bill Graham told the House of Commons that no decision had been made, when in fact it had, and the Americans were being informed of it.

The decision was finally leaked, presumably by the prime minister's office, on Tuesday evening to Radio-Canada. The story was confirmed to Canadian Press by an unnamed federal official. "[The Americans] were told we will not participate," the source said. "It is a firm 'no'. I am not sure it is an indefinite 'no.'"

According to the *Ottawa Citizen*, senior officials in Mr. Martin's office repeatedly denied persistent rumours in the days following that the Americans had been informed on Tuesday. Finally, on Thursday, a senior official in foreign affairs confirmed that the government had made up its mind the previous week that Mr. Pettigrew would deliver the news to the Americans of Canada's decision to not participate in missile defence at the NATO summit.

On Wednesday, February 23, the day the government released its budget, the prime minister told the House that "The government has stated all along that it will make the decision when it is in Canada's interest to do so." Later, NDP foreign-affairs critic, Alexa McDonough, accused Martin of contempt of parliament, "when he pretended that the government had not yet made a decision on Canada's participation in missile defence when that was clearly not the truth."

That evening, the prime minister called U.S. ambassador Paul Cellucci and told him that the next day Canada would say "no" to missile defence.

On Thursday, February 24, Paul Martin informed his Cabinet at their meeting that morning, and Chief of Defence Staff Rick Hillier explained the decision to the U.S. Joint Chiefs of Staff, including news of the large increase in defence spending provided by the budget.

Pierre Pettigrew made the first official announcement to a near-empty chamber in the House of Commons during a speech about the budget. Later, Martin made his brief announcement outside his office.

The American reaction was delivered by a "perplexed" Ambassador Cellucci, "We really don't get it," he said. "I personally don't think it's in Canada's sovereign interest to be outside the room when a decision is being made about a missile that might be coming toward Canada."

The ambassador reportedly added that not participating could result in the U.S. breaching Canada's airspace to intercept an incoming missile. "We will deploy. We will defend North America," he said. Martin shot back that he would insist that Canada would have to be involved in any decision to shoot down a missile in Canadian airspace.

But on this it must be pointed out that having Canada "in the room" when a decision was being made to shoot down a missile was never being offered by the United States. That decision fell to the U.S.-only Northern Command. Furthermore, the system is designed to intercept incoming missiles in the vacuum of space well beyond the edge of Canadian airspace, and hence outside of any claim of national sovereignty, since space is a global commons not subject to any nation's control.

In the weeks that followed, the fact that Bush would not return the prime minister's personal call to inform him of the decision before it was announced, and, later, Condoleezza Rice's delay of an intended visit to Ottawa, were taken as signs of the Bush administration's displeasure.

Eventually Martin would speak to Bush on the phone, and a White House spokesperson said, "The president expressed his understanding of the prime minister's decision, but underscored the importance of redoubling our security co-operation efforts [and] both leaders expressed the importance of our ongoing co-operation in NORAD to continental security."

Martin told reporters, "In terms of BMD, I pointed out, and the president agreed, that when you take a look at the increase in our defence budget and the very clear statement by Canada that we were going to defend the northern half of North America ... we're obviously going to cooperate in terms of NORAD, which is very important."

Two weeks later Cellucci, who would soon finish his term as ambassador, accused Paul Martin of flip-flopping on missile defence, because the Americans had been told Canada would join. "We've been pretty much assured for a long time that Canada wanted to participate, that this was in Canada's sovereign interest to participate," he told CTV.

Martin defended himself by arguing there was never anything substantial to commit to. Martin described the BMD system as an "evolving program." "We didn't want to get involved in something today only to find the situation would be different in two or three years," he said.

But history will show that Paul Martin made the correct decision. At the Liberal convention the main resolution was withdrawn from a debate on the conference floor by the Young Liberals, but a similar resolution against missile defence received overwhelming support in a workshop, and one delegate who spoke in support of missile defence was booed.

The public supported the government's decision as well by a wide margin. A poll by Decima found that 57 percent of Canadians supported Paul Martin's decision, while less than half that number, 26 percent, opposed his decision.

In the days and weeks that followed, predictable complaints about the decision were heard from all of the predictable quarters. "Exceptionally poor leadership ... Canada will pay the price," said a *Globe and Mail* editorial. "The 'no' decision is a mistake," wrote CanWest columnist Barbara Yaffe. A "public policy disaster," said the Conference of Defence Associations. "Canadian Free Riders," charged the *Wall Street Journal*. "The business community is left to deal with the fallout of a chilled relationship," complained the head of the Canadian Chamber of Commerce, pointing to a poll that showed 85 percent of CEOs surveyed felt the decision would be a "serious barrier to trade."

But there was no "missile trade war" as the *National Post* had predicted. NORAD continues to watch the skies, and billions of dollars in trade continues to move back and forth over the border. Canadians were just never convinced that there was a missile threat to Canada, nor did they trust the Americans either to resist using the system for nefarious purposes or to resolve long-standing "trade irritants" just because Canada agreed to co-operate on an unrelated military issue.

And in this case, there was ample evidence to show that a shoestring campaign by a handful of activists, experts, diplomats, and like-minded politicians from multiple parties turned this issue around. We were correct in our assumption when we started the campaign that the more Canadians learned about the system, the more they would become opposed.

Pollster Keith Neuman of Environics, which had been tracking the missile-defence issue since 2000, told the *Ottawa Citizen* that the majority of Canadians supported missile defence in 2000. Support waned slightly before the terrorist attacks of September 11, 2001, but increased afterwards. By 2002 a slight majority continued to support it, but this support was on the decline.

The key time period, according to Neuman, was between June and December of 2004—which also happened to be the most active period of our campaign. By December only four in ten Canadians supported missile defence, and during that time, "directed opinion," which means that Canadians felt strongly opposed to the issue, was strengthening.

Neuman claimed the lack of a champion who could explain the system's benefits was the problem, though I don't know what he thought Bill Graham and a host of other corporate and military leaders, backed by all of the editorial boards, were doing during that time. There seemed to be plenty of "champions" around.

In the absence of this leadership, according to Neuman, our campaign was able to come to dominate the debate. "Opposition to missile defence has been getting a great deal of media attention," wrote the *Citizen*, citing retired General Gard's high-profile visit as an example.

"Most of the press has been negative," he added. "It ties into Canadian discomfort with U.S. foreign policy. Unlike Americans, Canadians do not feel threatened by missiles from other countries ... People feel there should be cooperation on security in general. But this is different because it involves missiles and, potentially, weaponization of space. From the average Canadian point of view, it's not clear what it would do for Canada."

And here, I think he is absolutely correct. Our campaign was successful because we were able to build upon a set of fundamental Canadian values—co-operative and anti-militaristic values—that are shared by a great majority of Canadians in every part of the country.

At the root of the missile-defence issue was choice between two views: one believed that the rest of the world is a frightening and dangerous place from which we need to be protected; the other held that we should not be afraid, and instead play an important role in making the world a better place for everyone. Missile defence was symbolic of the darker outlook and Canadians rejected it and said they want to find a better, more Canadian, way.

AFTERWORD

THE END OF THIS ROUND

I began this book with an observation: Ever since there have been missiles, people have tried to build missile defences. And ever since the Americans have tried to build missile defences, there have been Canadians wanting to help them.

So far missile-defence opponents have successfully kept Canada from joining U.S. plans. But the United States has not given up on its missile-defence system, despite the missed deadlines, cost overruns, and poor performance. Nor has the missile-defence lobby in Canada given up; it continues to unabashedly urge the government to overturn Martin's decision.

Following that decision, Stephen Harper's Conservatives pledged that, if elected, they would reopen talks with the United States. Within a year, Harper was repeating his pledge during the January 2006 election campaign. If asked by the Americans, he said, he would return to the table and put a deal before parliament for a free vote.

In response, during the election a number of people involved in the Canadian Campaign to Oppose Missile Defence came together to compose a response to Harper. Our article, signed by me, former foreign affairs minister Lloyd Axworthy, Nobel Prize–winning chemist John Polanyi, Mel Hurtig, and many others, appeared in the *Toronto Star*.

We argued that "Canada was correct not to join missile defence in 2005, and nothing new has occurred that warrants reopening the debate." We pointed out that serious flaws remain in the system and costs are mounting. "News and analysis from the United States shows Canada to be vindicated, as it appears that confidence in the viability of the ground-based, mid-course system is faltering."

Later I was invited by *Globe and Mail* columnist Jeffrey Simpson to participate in a panel before his class of law students at the University of Ottawa. The other panellist was missile-defence proponent Derek H. Burney, former Canadian ambassador to the United States and Brian Mulroney's former chief of staff. Not surprisingly, Burney railed against Martin's decision and argued forcefully that Canada should join missile defence.

Stephen Harper won the January 2006 election, albeit with a minority. He is surrounded by missile-defence supporters, including Mr. Burney, who led Harper's transition team as they moved into the prime minister's office.

Burney continues to work behind the scenes in the Harper government. He and Harper's chief of staff, Ian Brodie, flew to Washington to speak with Bush administration officials to put Canada–U.S. relations back on an even keel prior to a summit of Harper, Bush, and Mexico's President Fox. Later, in what was described as an unprecedented and unexpected development, Burney and Brodie had a private meeting with President Bush. There's little doubt that Canada's contribution to missile defence was included in the discussions.

With the Conservatives in office, missile-defence proponents must not become complacent. Our victory was not total, and NORAD's connection with missile defence leaves a back door open for further Canadian participation.

For instance, Raytheon Corporation, one of the main American contractors for the missile shield, sent representatives to Goose Bay, Labrador, in 2005 to scout it as a possible location for a radar site. The Conservatives could attempt to justify the radar as coming under NORAD, but the system being proposed, called an X-Band radar, was designed by the U.S. Missile Defense Agency for the express purpose of assisting the missile shield.

This means that, even without a written agreement with the

Americans and a high-profile debate, the Conservatives could involve Canada largely by stealth if there is no vigilant public to keep a watchful eye and raise the alarm on any further contribution to the missile-defence system.

* * *

Following Paul Martin's announcement that Canada would not join missile defence, we thought it was important to hold a celebration of the campaign's success and mark this important moment, as well as to recognize those who had a hand in making history.

We invited our friends to join us for a party at the National Press Club, across the street from Parliament Hill. Leaders of citizen organizations and activists came together with members of parliament from three of the four parties: NDP leader Jack Layton and Alexa McDonough, the Bloc Québécois's Francine Lalonde and Claude Bachand, Liberals Bonnie Brown and Lynn Myers, as well as the now-Independent Carolyn Parrish. Denise Brunsdon from the Young Liberals of Canada came too.

Reflecting on that evening, I see now how unique our campaign was, for there were like-minded MPs from three different parties along with citizen activists—all celebrating a common victory. These moments do not occur very often.

Today, many of our small band of people involved in the Canadian Campaign to Oppose Missile Defence continue working on this and other, related, issues. A good part of my time is divided between limiting Canada's counter-terrorism role in Afghanistan and the logical follow-up to the missile-defence campaign, which is to encourage Canadian leadership in preventing the weaponization of space. Ceasefire.ca engages nearly twenty-five thousand people in ongoing peace and disarmament campaigns.

As a result of our campaign, Canada has retained the moral authority to take up disarmament issues like nuclear and space weapons. That is why we worked so hard to keep Canada out of missile defence—so that Canadians could proudly say that we will decide our own role in the world.

Sure, we live next door to the world's last superpower, and have many close relationships with the American people—but sometimes we will disagree with their government.

Canadian values are very strong. That's why in the face of so many bad decisions made by our government, I am sometimes a pessimist about tomorrow—but I'm always an optimist about the day after.

TIMELINE

1944	The missile age begins when German V-2 missiles strike London during the Second World War.
1945	
July 16	The nuclear age begins when the U.S. conducts Trinity, the first test of an atomic bomb.
August 6, 9	The U.S. drops atomic bombs on Hiroshima and Nagasaki, killing more than 200,000 Japanese.
1949	The Soviet Union tests its first nuclear bomb.
1952	Britain tests its first nuclear bomb.
1957	The Soviet Union tests its first Inter-Continental Ballistic Missile (ICBM); two months later it launches Sputnik, the world's first satellite.
	The Distant Early Warning (DEW) Line of radars from Baffin Island to Alaska become operational.
	The first satellite-tracking camera is operated by the U.S.
	The U.S. launches its first ICBM.
1958	The United States decides to establish a Ballistic Missile Early Warning System (BMEWS).
	North American Air Defense Command (NORAD) officially assumes control of Canadian and U.S. air defences against Soviet bombers.
	The U.S. begins work on its first anti-missile system, Nike Zeus.
1960	France tests its first nuclear bomb.
	The U.S.'s first BMEWS radar capable of tracking mis-

siles become operational in Thule, Greenland.
NORAD begins monitoring satellites and missiles in space.

1961   The Soviets conduct their first successful missile intercept using an anti-ballistic missile (ABM) system.
A second BMEWS radar becomes operational in Alaska

1962   The U.S. conducts a "close enough" missile intercept test of the Nike Zeus ABM missile interceptor.

1963   The Limited Test Ban Treaty is signed by the Soviet Union, Britain, and the U.S., prohibiting the testing of nuclear weapons above ground, under water, or in space.
Prime Minister Lester B. Pearson agrees to allow BOMARC missiles in Canada to be nuclear-armed.

1964   China tests its first nuclear bomb.
Russia begins deployment of an ABM system to defend Moscow.
The U.S.'s third BMEWS radar becomes operational in Fylingsdale, U.K.

1966   China launches its first nuclear-tipped missile.
NORAD moves to its new nuclear-attack-proof underground Cheyenne Mountain complex.

1967   U.S. announces it will pursue its Sentinel ABM system (successor to Nike), including 700 interceptors.
Russia, the U.S., and dozens of others sign the Outer Space Treaty, banning nuclear weapons and weapons of mass destruction from orbit.

1968   Canada renews the NORAD agreement with the U.S., but with a caveat that Canada will not participate in active ballistic-missile defence (BMD).
Nuclear and non-nuclear weapon states sign the Nuclear Non-Proliferation Treaty (NPT) limiting the spread of nuclear weapons.

1969   President Nixon scales back deployment of controversial Sentinel system and renames it Safeguard.

1971	A U.S. Defense Support Program satellite conducts its first orbit, providing space-based missile early warning.
1972	The Soviet Union and the U.S. sign the Anti-Ballistic Missile Treaty (ABM).
1974	India tests its first nuclear bomb clandestinely, but does not develop more weapons.
1975	An updated NORAD agreement acknowledges its role in space surveillance and aerospace to warn of a missile attack, as well as bomber attacks.
	The U.S.'s Safeguard system becomes operational in North Dakota, but is deactivated after 133 days because of cost and ineffectiveness.
	NORAD's name is changed from "air defense" to "aerospace defense," and Canada's no-BMD caveat is dropped from the agreement.
1983	President Ronald Reagan announces the Strategic Defense Initiative (SDI), later dubbed "Star Wars" by opponents.
1985	Prime Minister Brian Mulroney announces Canada's decision to decline the invitation to participate in SDI.
1991	The Soviet Union officially dissolves.
	The Bush administration scales back SDI due to cost, technology, and the end of the Cold War, to focus on a limited, ABM Treaty–compliant system.
1993	President Bill Clinton declares "the end of the Star Wars era" and focuses on limited, battlefield missile defences.
1996	The Clinton administration creates a three-year National Missile Defense test program, which could lead to deployment within an additional three years.
1998	India, followed by Pakistan, tests nuclear bombs.
	North Korea fails in an attempt to launch a satellite.
1999	Under pressure, Clinton signs the National Missile Defense Act, calling for deployment "as soon as technically possible."

After negotiations, North Korea agrees to suspend missile testing.

NMD has a successful intercept test, but later a contractor is accused of falsifying test data.

Canadian delegation visiting U.S. labs is told research would begin on space weapons.

2000   The second NMD test fails to intercept the target.

Presidential candidate George W. Bush pledges to deploy a missile-defence system to defend against rogue nations and accidental attacks.

The third NMD test fails when the kill vehicle does not separate from its booster.

Clinton defers a decision to deploy the NMD system to his successor.

2001   The new Bush administration requests $8.3 billion for missile defence (Congress approves $7.8 billion).

The fourth NMD test is deemed a success.

September 11 Terrorists strike the World Trade Center and Pentagon with hijacked passenger jets.

The fifth NMD test is deemed successful.

Bush announces the U.S. will withdraw from the ABM treaty six months later—in June 2002.

2002   U.S. Defense Secretary Donald Rumsfeld creates the Missile Defense Agency and embarks on an ambitious, layered missile-defence system "against all ranges of threats."

March   The sixth missile defence test is deemed successful.

June   The seventh missile-defence test is successful when a ship-launched missile intercepts its target.

December   The eighth missile defence test fails when the kill vehicle fails to separate from the booster once again.

December 17 President Bush orders the deployment of a missile defence system, starting with up to 20 ground-based missile interceptors in Alaska, "Today I am pleased to announce we will take another important step in countering these threats by beginning to field missile defense capabilities to protect the United States as well as our friends and allies."

2003

January   Defence Minister John McCallum discusses BMD with Rumsfeld in Washington.

Foreign Affairs Minister Bill Graham expresses concern over weaponization of space.

Delegation of foreign affairs and defence officials goes to Washington for missile-defence talks.

March 17   Prime Minister Jean Chrétien announces that Canada will not participate in the invasion of Iraq.

April   Liberal-leadership candidate Paul Martin tells reporters he favours Canada joining the U.S. missile-defence program.

"Say No to Missile Defence" column by Lloyd Axworthy and Michael Byers appears in *Globe and Mail*.

U.S. Air Force chief says allies will have "no veto" over missile-defence programs, such as space-based weapons.

May   Denmark allows the U.S. to upgrade the radar in Thule, Greenland, for missile defence use.

Graham says Canada will raise its opposition to space weapons during U.S. talks.

Aerospace corporations urge Chrétien to join missile defence in order to win U.S. military contracts.

McCallum and Graham tell the Liberal Caucus and Parliament that NORAD is at risk and there may be only 100 days to join missile defence.

SES/Sun Media poll finds 61 percent favour "participating in a space-based defence shield."

May 30   McCallum announces the commencement of formal discussions with the U.S. on joining missile defence.

June   38 Liberal MPs vote against a Canadian Alliance motion supporting missile defence, and Martin avoids the vote.

July	McCallum has a "good discussion" with Rumsfeld on missile defence.
	U.S. NORAD commander says the sooner Canada joins, the sooner companies will see benefits.
	McCallum predicts Cabinet could decide on an agreement to join "by the fall."
September	After three official meetings, McCallum thinks fall decision is possible.
November 15	Paul Martin wins Liberal Party leadership race.
	Pollara poll finds 64 percent favour Canadian participation in U.S. NORTHCOM.
December	Australia agrees to join missile defence.
	The Conservative Party is formed from a merger of the Canadian Alliance and the Progressive Conservatives.
	Paul Martin becomes prime minister and appoints his first Cabinet.
2004	
January	Prime Minister Martin meets with President Bush and hemispheric leaders in Mexico.
	Defence Minister David Pratt says decision must be made by October when U.S. system is operational.
January 15	Pratt writes to Rumsfeld seeking talks for "Canada's closest possible involvement in missile defence."
February	No "show stoppers" in missile defence talks, says Lt. Gen Findley, chief Canadian at NORAD.
	Russia says its new missile can make "any missile defence useless."
	Pratt accuses NDP, BQ of looking "too far ahead" at possible weaponization of space.
	30 Liberal MPs vote for BQ motion against joining missile defence.
March	The Canadian Campaign to Oppose Missile Defence is formed and releases its "Stars Against Star Wars" open letter to Paul Martin.
April	Internal DND report warns that BMD reinforces trend

to "weaponization of outer space."

U.S. Government Accounting Office says government has no understanding of full cost or capability of BMD system.

May	Paul Martin calls election for June 28, 2004.
June	NDP features missile defence in election ads.
	Anti-BMD day of protest in ten cities across Canada.
	Layton clashes with Martin on BMD in English TV debate.
June 28	Liberals win June 28 election with minority of seats.
July	The U.S. Missile Defense Agency installs the first interceptor missile in Alaska.
	Martin informs the U.S. that Canada will agree to NORAD amendment allowing data to be shared with U.S. missile-shield command.
	U.S. Ambassador Paul Cellucci urges Canada to join missile defence to strengthen NORAD, ensure security.
	Bill Graham replaces Pratt as defence minister; takes over BMD file.
August 5	NORAD amended to share missile-warning and tracking data with U.S. Northern Command, which is responsible for operating the continental missile defence system.
	Foreign Affairs Minister Pierre Pettigrew promises "input from Parliament" on missile defence decision.
	Conservative defence critic Gordon O'Connor says "we are neither for nor against it until we get the details."
	U.S. Lt. Gen. (ret.) Robert Gard, Jr., tells Ottawa the system is unproven, expensive, and may never work.
	Layton warns Martin that NDP will not compromise on missile defence.
	Liberal MP Carolyn Parrish says that Canada should not join the "coalition of the idiots" in missile defence
September	Some Liberal MPs suggest waiting for U.S. election before making missile defence decision.

238   MISSILE DEFENCE

Graham argues joining missile defence is important for
Canada–U.S. relations

October   MIT Professor Ted Postol tells Ottawa that missile-
defence system "can never work."

"Small but colourful" demonstrations in 30 cities on
eve of Parliament's resumption.

Conservatives force Liberals to put commitment of a
missile-defence vote in Throne Speech.

EKOS poll for DND finds 54 percent favour missile
defence talks and 40 percent oppose, but support is
declining.

November 2   George W. Bush defeats Democratic challenger John
Kerry in U.S. presidential election.

SES Research polls finds 56 percent somewhat/strongly
oppose missile defence; CRIC poll finds 52 percent
oppose it.

Russian President Putin says Russia is developing new
nuclear missile.

Martin dismisses Parrish from Liberal caucus after more
remarks.

November 30   During official visit, Bush unexpectedly raises missile
defence during Ottawa press conference.

December 1   Bush asks Canada to join missile defence in Halifax
speech.

Aftermath of Bush visit puts missile defence at top of
the political, media agenda.

Liberals' Quebec wing passes motion calling on government not to join missile defence.

Chief of Defence Staff Gen. Ray Henault says NORAD
will endure, even if Canada says "no" to missile defence.

U.S. Ambassador (ret.) Jonathan Dean tells Ottawa that
missile defence will lead to weapons in space.

Martin says he wants to have influence and give no land
or money to join missile defence.

The ninth missile-defence test, the first in two years,

fails when ground-based interceptor malfunctions.
Layton says missile-defence vote could bring down
Liberal minority government.
Bush officially misses year-end goal to declare missile-
defence system operational.

2005
January   Cellucci says he hopes Canada will join BMD and was
             told decision coming "over the next couple of months."
             Polaris Institute report questions Frank McKenna's
             appointment as ambassador to the U.S. over links to
             Bush family, investments.
             Canadian ambassador to U.S. Michael Kergin says gov-
             ernment needs more information on influence over
             missile defence.
             Graham denies U.S. pressuring Canada at Liberal
             Caucus in Fredericton.
February   New York conference argues missile defence has been
             wrongly linked to space weapons.
             Graham denies missile defence is a dead issue.
             Cellucci says it's in Canada's "sovereign interest" to join
             missile defence.
             EKOS/*Toronto Star* poll finds 54 per cent oppose missile
             defence, two-thirds consider it an election issue.
             Tenth missile-defence test is a failure when the ground-
             based interceptor fails to launch.
             Anti-missile-defence resolution to go to vote at Liberal
             Party convention March 3–6 in Ottawa.
February 22 Pettigrew informs U.S. Sec. of State Condoleezza Rice
             that Canada will not join BMD.
             New Canadian ambassador to U.S., McKenna, tells
             reporters Canada is already "part of" missile defence.
             Graham tells Parliament that "we have yet to make any
             decisions in terms of missile defence."
             Radio Canada reports that according to a source, Martin
             will say no to BMD.

February 23   Federal budget includes $12.8-billion boost to military
                spending over five years.

                Wednesday night, Martin informs Cellucci that Canada
                will announce his "no" decision on Thursday.

February 24   Martin informs his Cabinet of his decision to not join
                BMD.

                Canadian Chief of Defence Staff Gen. Rick Hillier
                informs U.S. joint chiefs.

                Pettigrew announces in parliament that Canada will not
                join missile defence.

                Martin announces to reporters that "Canada will not
                take part in the proposed BMD system."

                Cellucci quips about Canadian decision, "we don't get
                it."

February 25   Martin says Canada would have to give permission
                before missile could be fired over Canada.

                NDP and Conservatives complain that BMD decision
                was not brought to a vote.

                Graham denies missile defence decision has harmed
                U.S. relations.

                Missile-defence lobby decries decision, predicts trade
                problems, end of NORAD.

March   Rice, disappointed over the BMD decision, informs
                Pettigrew that she will delay her Ottawa visit.

                White House spokesperson expresses disappointment,
                but says governments are moving forward.

                Liberal delegates back Martin's BMD decision at con-
                vention.

                Bush returns Martin's call to discuss BMD decision, says
                he accepts decision.

                Cellucci accuses Martin of reneging, saying U.S. had
                been "assured" of participation.

                Martin says Canada never got clear answers on what
                participation would entail.

                Lt.-Gen. Findlay, top Canadian at NORAD, says "nothing has fundamentally changed at NORAD."

Conservative Party leader Stephen Harper pledges to return to negotiating table if the Conservatives win the next election.

Decima poll finds 57 percent in favour of BMD decision, a majority citing concern about Bush as a major factor.

June   Raytheon Corporation scouts Goose Bay, Nfld., as a location for a missile defence X-Band radar site.

2006   The Conservatives pledge to reopen missile defence talks if asked by the U.S.

January   Conservatives win federal election and form a minority government.

MEMBER OF SCABRINI GROUP

Québec, Canada
2006